Stressfire II

by
Massad F. Ayoob

Available from   *Police Bookshelf*
                 P.O. Box 122
                 Concord, N.H. 03301 USA

2nd Printing, 1993

ISBN 0-936279-11-7

DEDICATION

Certain professionals more than others have helped the author better understand the combat dynamics and forensic dynamics of shotguns wounds to the human body. This book is respectfully dedicated to Lt. Cmdr. Vernon Geberth, NYPD Bronx Homicide Task Force (Ret.); Master Evidence Technician and SWAT Trainer Alan Kulovitz of the Cook County (Ill.) Sheriff's Dept.; Lt. Chuck Higbie, LAPD OIS Unit Commander (Ret.); Sgt. Dave Trahin, LAPD Firearms Examination Unit (Ret.); and especially Doctors Joseph Davis, Martin Fackler, Valerie Rao, and Charles Wetli. This book is dedicated to these fine men and women, in hopes that in some small way it can contribute to their personal goals of reducing violent deaths of the innocent.

Massad Ayoob
Concord, NH
1992

Foreword

by Ed Nowicki

The shotgun in law enforcement may be one of the most under used, yet effective firearms available. So, it seems quite fitting that one of the nation's leading law enforcement firearms trainers, Massad Ayoob, has finally written a book that addresses the tactical use of the shotgun for law enforcement in such an enlightening and practical manner. The research and extensive effort that Mas put into this book, make for one of the best books that I have ever read on use of the shotgun for law enforcement. He is widely respected as one of law enforcement's most gifted and talented firearms writers.

A number of years ago, I had the opportunity to meet the man that I had heard so much about, and whose writings I read for many years. I discovered, like most other law enforcement officers who got to know Massad Ayoob, that he is a "straight shooter' with more than his considerable shooting ability. He is driven in his efforts to show law enforcement officers how to survive the streets and the courts in the best ways possible. After that meeting, I realized that Mas genuinely cares about how he trains and what he writes. From that day on, I also had the opportunity to call him my friend.

Those of us who know Massad Ayoob also know that if his name is listed as the author of a book or an article, that the book or article is must reading. His considerable influence in the law enforcement community is witnessed by the fact that he has personally recruited more than ten-percent of the members in the nation's largest law enforcement training organization: the American Society of Law Enforcement Trainers (ASLET). His firearms training programs are filled to capacity and he has helped many officers survive the courts through his courtroom skills as an articulate and knowledgeable expert witness on the use of lethal force. If I were ever in need of an expert witness on the use of lethal force, Massad would stand alone at the top of that list.

There are not too many individuals in this nation who possess the tactical ability, shooting skills and writing skills to write a comprehensive book on the shotgun as a self-defense firearm for law enforcement - Massad Ayoob is one of them, and what a book he has written! This is a book by an experienced law enforcement officer who also has the opportunity to interact with some of the most tactically skilled officers around the nation. I have no doubts that this book will be referred to as a "classic" police shotgun book in the years ahead.

The pages in front of you are much more than a book, they are an important part of a comprehensive shotgun training program. You may think that you know how to work a shotgun, but do you know how a shotgun really works? There is a difference. In fact, when I was involved in one of the six shooting incidents in my law enforcement career, I shot an individual with a 12 gauge shotgun after he confronted me with a double-barreled sawed-off 12 gauge. Fortunately, I survived this incident and the experience made me a believer in the effectiveness of the shotgun. Even though I survived, I wish that I would have had the opportunity to have read this book before the incident. I was lucky!

This book is the shotgun equivalent of Mas's highly acclaimed and "must read" book on realistic handgun shooting titled, StressFire. I have no doubt that StressFire has kept many law enforcement officers alive. I am also sure that this book will also prevent many future injuries and deaths to our great nation's crime fighters.

If you want to understand the purpose of the police shotgun, you don't want to read this book, you want to absorb it. It's that kind of book. When you think that you know its contents, read it again and you will learn more. Remember, what you learn today can keep you alive tomorrow.

Ed Nowicki
Twin Lakes, WI

Author's Note: A survivor of six separate shooting incidents, Ed Nowicki was for many years the Executive Director of the nation's largest law enforcement training association, the prestigious American Society of Law Enforcement Trainers (ASLET). He is one of the nation's top law enforcement trainers, a widely published author and a judicially recognized expert on law enforcement training and education.

Table of Contents

Chapter 1

The Purpose of This Book

If you read "StressFire" (1983) you understand what happens to the body in times of stress that is sufficiently life-threatening that you need a gun in your hand. You will experience the very height of body alarm reaction, known as "fight or flight reflex."

Occurring in all mammals and representing the epitome of what a layman would call "survival instinct," the fight or flight response was first quantified by Dr. Walter Cannon at Harvard Medical School at the dawn of the Twentieth Century. Epinephrine ("adrenaline") and norepinephrine will be instantly released by the adrenal system. There is no ninety seconds required for anything to go through the circulatory system. The adrenal dump takes place immediately.

The body will shut down its pain receptor/response system to a large degree. This is why men in fights do not feel pain (at the time) from the blows they receive, and why they even sustain gunshot and knife wounds without being aware of them until later.

There will be a period of virtually superhuman strength. This is what accounts for the documentable cases of frail grandmothers lifting automobiles from atop their grandchildren...and for men shot nine or ten or twenty times with powerful pistol bullets to keep advancing, pulling their own triggers. True, the grandmother will tear loose every muscle in her back and perhaps suffer one or more compression fractures of her spine from the Herculean effort, but her immediate goal of rescue will have been achieved. True, the armed opponent may literally be shot to pieces with irreparable wounds that will cause his death in seconds, but in those seconds, he will fulfill

1

his determination to commit murder if not stopped.

Where does the defensive combat shotgun come in? It is understood that the same fight or flight reflex experienced by the defender is happening to the aggressor, making *him* stronger, faster, harder and more impervious to pain. This means that to be sure of stopping his actions in time, a more destructive and powerful wounding mechanism enhances the defender's chances of survival.

Locked into the body at one end, a properly fitted shotgun is much steadier to hold than a pistol. One downside of fight or flight reflex is the dramatic fine-motor tremor that tends to occur in the body, striking the extremities — the hands — first. A seven-pound shotgun locked in tight at one end to the torso will be far less likely to tremor off target than a pistol extended at the end of a shaky arm.

An effect of the survival instinct is tunnel vision, which occurs through cortical perception. The cortex of the brain, in survival mode, screens out anything it does not instinctively recognize as critical to escaping or neutralizing the killing threat. Because the gun came too late to the epoch of Man for instincts to develop around it, this means gunsights will often be forgotten.

The pistol, with its short overall length, is extremely difficult to align with a target with a "natural point," and if the eyes are no longer correlating the gunsights, the defending pistol shots are now likely to miss. This is why in the StressFire system we emphasize the StressPoint Index or Sightpoint Index, in which the barrel of the gun and its sights are forced into the cone of tunnel vision to achieve a crudely efficient alignment.

The shotgun works much better for this, since its fat, long barrel extends more easily to eye level when it has been mounted to the chest. This is why shooters of both clay birds and feathered ones can blast them out of the air in flight without concentrating on sight alignment. This principle is most advantageous in fight or flight situations.

However, many sporting shotgun techniques have failed when, as has been customary, they are adapted to defensive shooting. The human body, when threatened, does not care to blade itself the way a sport-trained shotgunner is trained to position his torso vis-a-vis the target. Dr. Cannon and his followers noted that the head would turn instantly toward the threat, and we know now that a principle of human physiology is that "where the head turns, the body follows." The defensive shooter in the grip of survival instinct winds up with his torso square with the threat. Cannon and his followers observed the same in all bipedal mammals: Man, the primates, even a bear on his hind legs. If the defending human has not been taught to wield a shotgun from this position, the shot will tend to go left far enough to

2

miss a human target, when fired by a right-handed defender.

Cannon also noted that the body would crouch. This term has been widely misunderstood by gun people with limited knowledge of physiology. The crouch as defined by Cannon is not a wide-straddled squat as commonly depicted in gun books. This position compromises both balance and mobility, and does not occur in nature. Rather, the shoulders will come somewhat forward of the hips; the knees will flex, usually to a limited degree, to "coil" the limbs for powerful and sudden movement in any direction; and the head will come forward as the shoulders slightly hunch upward as if to protect the skull.

All these physiological truths have been incorporated into the StressFire advanced combat shotgun system. As with the handgun version, the principle was to determine through consultation with physicians, psychiatrists, and physiologists what would happen to the human being with a specific weapon in hand when this effect struck, and then to backspace and create techniques that could be trained into the individual...techniques that not only would not break under stress, but which would actually feed off the gross strength increase of the fight or flight reflex and become even stronger in the moment of truth.

These techniques have been tested in the field by some of our graduates. They have worked every bit as well as we have hoped, and at this writing the shotgun StressFire principles have helped to save the lives of seven police officers and one hostage, all of whom emerged from their "kill or die" conflicts unscathed, which cannot be said for the murderous offenders (four dead on scene, one D.O.A., one paralyzed).

When I quantified the initial StressFire concept in the early 1980's, I never dreamed that by the end of the decade it would be adopted by the United States Army to form the core of their new combat pistolcraft doctrine, as distilled into their manual FM 23-35. I only hoped that it would preserve the lives of the innocent. This it has done — a much more satisfying accolade — and the advanced combat shotgun techniques of StressFire II have already done the same.

My job was developing and quantifying the techniques, and showing the Good Guys how to implement them and train with them to make them function reflexively in times of crisis. Your job is to determine if they'll work for you, and then absorb them. No book will do that for you by itself.

Chapter 2

Why the Combat Shotgun?

The shotgun has been successfully used by American and Canadian police, by armed citizens the world over, and by many armies' jungle warfare troops and military police. The reasons why boil down to these two: for the properly trained person, *the shotgun is easy to hit with under stress* and, within its range and when properly loaded, *the shotgun can deliver massive stopping power against persons and mammals that are in the grip of "fight or flight reflex" or rage response.*

Shotgun Hit Potential

It is understood in marksmanship that long guns, rifles and shotguns, are easier to hit the target with than pistols or revolvers. Additionally, the widening charge of shot fired from the "scattergun" makes precise aim less important at certain distances. With less time required to aim, the shotgun can be fired more rapidly at single *or* multiple targets, and it will be more forgiving in terms of hit potential. For example, an armed felon fifteen yards away pivots toward you, presenting his right side as he aims his pistol at you, and you jerk the trigger, pulling the muzzle sideways. Your aim has been disturbed sufficiently that your bullet merely plucks at his shirt as it passes harmlessly in front of his chest. If you had fired a shotgun loaded with standard 00 buckshot in exactly the same way, probably four of the nine .33 caliber lead projectiles would have pierced his chest.

Combat competition clearly shows the shotgun's advantage over

Shotgun's firepower is apparent in this photo. S&W model 3913 pistol needs 8 separate pulls of the trigger to deliver 8 .36-calibar bullets at 1300 feet per second, and hot ammo to boot. A standard pressure round of 000 buckshot delivers the same 8 36-caliber projectiles at 1300 fps or better velocity with a single pull of the trigger.

the handgun in multiple target scenarios at the realistic distance of 25 feet or so. Firing at five bowling pins, a shooter who blows them all away in four to five seconds with a .45 caliber pistol will probably accomplish the same task in between 2.0 and 2.5 seconds with a semiautomatic shotgun.

Common sense shows us that with the single-projectile rifled slug load, *for most users*, the shotgun's practical range will also exceed that of the handgun. We note that the average sportsman is quite capable of hunting deer with a 12-gauge in shotgun-only wildlife areas, while it takes a superb pistol shot to hunt the same game in similar areas. The most avid handgun aficionado will admit that hunting with pistols requires an extremely high skill level because it is much more difficult than doing so with a rifle or shotgun, and many sportsmen consider handgun hunting to be a "stunt."

Extrapolating this to the situation of a police manhunt in a wooded area where confrontation distance may range from contact to fifty or a hundred yards, and we see that the slug-loaded shotgun

Chief Russell Lary, left, and Captain Massad Ayoob are satisfied with the weapons in each of their department's police cars: one Ruger Mini-14 .223 semiautomatic rifle *and* one Benelli Super-90 12-gauge semiautomatic shotgun per cruiser.

gives its user greater hit potential. Even in urban confrontations, the buckshot-loaded 12 gauge improves hit potential. In the early 1980s, LAPD determined that 28% of the shots fired in combat by officers with double action .38 Special revolvers struck the offender, while 58% of the 00 buckshot rounds fired from their cruiser-standard Ithaca shotguns scored hits. It should be noted, however, that LAPD has traditionally spent more training time on the shotgun than most police departments.

The shotgun's reputation for stopping power will be discussed in a subsequent chapter.

The shotgun is not, however, the perfect close-range antipersonnel weapon for every situation. Many users do not have the training to manage its notoriously vicious recoil...the combat shotgun's versatility has been somewhat exaggerated...and being a two-handed weapon, it limits the ability of the user to employ one arm for balance, communication, door-opening, or illumination. Similarly, it is far from the easiest weapon to return fire with if one arm is injured or otherwise occupied.

This book will be aimed at maximizing the individual's ability to control the combat shotgun in accurate rapid fire, in tactical situations, without pain or injury. As with all forms of training, we must take into account both the tool and the user, and assess the strengths as well as the weaknesses of both, so as to formulate both plans of action and inculcated skills that allow us to shore up the weaknesses while taking maximum advantages of the strengths.

Chapter 3

The Combat Shotgun Cartridge's Effect on Human Tissue

Massive stopping power is the *raison d'etre* of the combat shotgun. However, all shotgun shells are not created equal when it comes to performance in human flesh at various ranges. Depending on the load selected, one can go from impotence to overkill. Let us look at some of the rounds presently available.

Rubber projectiles. At very close range, these supposedly "non-lethal" rounds can still kill and, at considerably greater distance, can maim. The fact that one fired rubber balls would be seen by the courts as reason to believe that the shooter did not intend lethal force and did not feel killing or crippling level of injury was warranted. Having now delivered a deadly level of force, there is now almost prima facie evidence that even by the defendant's own standards, he caused more damage than he wanted to do or believed he was authorized to do. A verdict for manslaughter, aggravated assault, or wrongful death or injury is now virtually assured. *One should never use an inherently deadly weapon in an attempt to inflict a less than lethal injury.*

Gas projectiles. Typified by the outstanding AAI Ferret round, 12-gauge gas shells are available in both CN (tear gas) and CS (choking gas) formulations. While delivering far less payload than the standard 37mm. gas-gun shell, these are ideal for small, confined areas: mobile homes, vans, closets, etc. Since they are by definition "barricade-penetrating projectiles," they can of course kill if they strike at close range unimpeded by intervening targets. Good manners indicate that the medical examiner be furnished a gas mask. Ferret shells are very useful for police special response teams, but require gas masks for those who will go in to "mop up", are not guaranteed to incapacitate, and are of no use to armed citizens.

Mechanisms of Injury

Before going on with more conventional shotgun loads, it is useful to understand their wounding mechanisms. The relatively low-velocity rifled slug kills via an unusually wide and relatively deep "permanent crush cavity" of destroyed tissue. Multi-projectile shot cartridges will function via one of two dynamics: "tunnel wound effect" or "saturation effect."

Saturation effect takes place at distances where the shot pattern has had room to spread. Multiple organs, nerve complexes, blood vessels, and bones are struck simultaneously. This compounded damage will generally shut down an organism more rapidly than if a single organ was destroyed.

Tunnel wound effect, sometimes more graphically called "rat-hole wound effect," occurs when the range is so close that the shot charge strikes en masse. A huge tunnel is bored through flesh, destroying even more tissue in terms of permanent crush cavity than a slug, since the pattern is probably starting to spread and the ounce or so of lead shot strikes in an area wider than the fixed diameter of a rifled slug.

At close range, the wadding at the base of the shot charge (sometimes taking the form of a plastic sleeve that encompasses the charge lengthways) will be driven into the wound. At distances of seven yards or thereabouts, the wad will strike the target away from the shot entry holes, often with enough force to lacerate or bruise, sometimes even leaving a depressed injury. At closer range, it may be recovered from the corpse upon autopsy; having travelled directly behind the shot charge into tissue already destroyed, its presence will seldom magnify the injury and, in any case, will be the least of the patient's concerns. Indeed, it may have a benevolent effect. In one Illinois case, a downed police officer was shot in the neck at point blank range with a 12-gauge shotgun loaded with #6 birdshot. The tunnel wound effect created a two-inch diameter rat-hole through his neck, and the criminal who had shot him left the cop for dead upon observing the massive injury. The officer survived, however; the wadding that had followed the charge had miraculously blocked his lacerated carotid artery and kept him from bleeding to death. He has since recovered.

A phenomenon called "billiard ball effect" is often seen in shotgun pellet injuries. Though it can occur just in flesh, it will be more pronounced if the pellet charge has struck hard bone on its way into the body. The pellets will then carom outward, cutting a much wider swath of injury. The same can occur if the pellets have passed through a hard intermediate target — glass, for instance, or a hollow core door — prior to striking the subject.

Conventional Shotgun Loads

Many experts recommend *birdshot* for very close range work. The theory is that the tiny pellets, which decelerate quickly, will not go through house walls with enough force to kill family members in adjacent rooms. This is not necessarily true, and in any case, projectiles that would not go through a sheetrock wall (something easily accomplished with a human fist) will not reliably go into heavily-clad human bodies, either.

Some special reaction teams use tiny-pellet #9 or even finer #12 birdshot when raiding intensely-populated dwellings under circumstances that prohibit evacuation of adjacent rooms or apartments. On the questionable theory that the tiny pellets will not bounce with enough residual force to cause serious injury, some prison response teams use the same loads when entering individual cells where they believe the inhabitants may be armed with deadly weapons.

Since a shell that could not reliably neutralize a human being behind a sheetrock wall probably could not do the same to someone behind furniture, a home defense shotgun so loaded is now totally impotent against an armed intruder who ducks behind cover in a doorway or in back of a sofa. For this reason, the author uses buckshot in his home defense shotguns and in any police shotgun used for building searches.

Buckshot is the near-unanimous choice for man-size targets at ranges predictable at under 25 yards. Optimum range for maximum saturation effect is between ten and fifteen yards; 25 to 35 yards presents the outer limit of predictable neutralization of human targets; and close range destruction will equal or exceed that of the 12-bore slug.

At extended ranges, we have seen buckshot of all sizes fail to penetrate a cardboard target. Here, we are talking fifty yards or more. This is not to say that the buckshot-loaded weapon is not lethal at this distance, only that its lethality is unpredictable. One of the author's police graduates engaged a felon approximately 50 yards distant. They traded shots at each other, both firing 00 buck from l2-ga. shotguns, until the suspect broke off the attack and fled into a nearby swamp. He was found there dead, face down in the water, with a single .33 caliber pellet lodged inside his head.

In an infamous San Jose shooting, a deranged homeless man snatched a police officer's revolver, murdered him with it, then engaged other officers in a running gunfight. After he had been killed, another officer was found a block away dying. He was thought at first to have been slain by the cop killer with the stolen service revolver. However, autopsy showed that a single 00 buckshot pellet fired by another officer had gone past the offender and struck the officer, entering below his ballistic vest and severing the abdominal aorta. The dead officer was between 50 and 60 yards from the officer who fired.

As a general rule, heavier pellets will carry farther and penetrate more deeply. Thus, in winter when opponents are likely to be wearing heavy clothing that can quickly blunt the velocity of non-aerodynamic buckshot pellets, larger projectiles such as 00 or .36-caliber 000 pellets make sense, while in warm weather less penetrative smaller pellets with better saturation, like the .30 caliber #1 Buck, may be more desirable. Heavy clothing, as the photos show, reduces the likelihood of 00 type pellets overpenetrating the human body.

It must always be borne in mind that even massive saturation effect will not always immediately stop a determined aggressor, or one heavily under the influence of certain drugs. A member of the NYPD Stakeout Squad engaged a heroin addict who refused the command to drop his gun and was shot through the chest, front to back and left to right with nine 00 buck pellets at a range of less than seven yards. The armed man jerked violently backward, but instead of falling down, spun on his heel and ran and was shot again. He was seen to stumble but stay on his feet as the second full charge of buck drove back to front through his torso. The suspect made it to the door of the establishment where he was shot in the buttock by another officer with a low-velocity, mid range wadcutter .38 Special bullet weighing 148 grains. This bullet broke the pelvis and the suspect pitched forward through the automatically-opening door.

The first officer covered the fallen man with the shotgun only to see him push himself upward and aim his revolver at the cop. The patrolman fired a third round of 00 buck, all nine .33 pellets piercing deeply into the offender's torso even after smashing through the glass door that was starting to close behind him. The man jerked violently and flopped over, his gun flying away. The officer covered him as the suspect crawled to a nearby wall and pulled himself upward to a half-sitting position. "Don't shoot me, I'm on fire," the armed robbery suspect gurgled; the officer said he sounded like a man talking under water because his lungs were so full of blood. The man then slumped to the ground, his heart and thoracic viscera shredded, and was pronounced dead not long after arrival at the hospital. Note that he had remained a viable offender after 18 00 buckshot wounds and a .38 hit, and was able to perform dynamic although non-threatening motions after a total of 27 pellet wounds plus the handgun wound.

In another Stakeout Squad shooting, a left-handed suspect was shot through the upper torso, armpit to armpit, left to right as he pointed his revolver at the officers. The cop who fired vividly recalls seeing the man's feet in the air an instant after the shot.

The man fell heavily to his back, his gun landing on the floor a distance away, next to a second armed robber who had been killed outright by a second officer. Both cops watched as the man hit through the armpit got to his feet and staggered out the door. The officers, guns at the ready, followed him cautiously; because he had dropped his weapon, they did not fire again. The man staggered a full city block before collapsing unconscious; the officers described him as walking like a zombie. The suspect was transported by ambulance.

A Stakeout sergeant told me that he and the involved officer responded to the hospital within an hour, hoping to get a dying statement from the man. The sergeant said they entered the examination room to find the suspect on his back with the surgeon probing the entry wound with two gloved fingers. The suspect, upon seeing them, pulled himself upright (with the doctor's fingers still inside his chest) and cried accusingly, "Hey! You the motherfucker shot me!"

The robber survived to stand trial. The one-ounce, .72 caliber slug had entered high in the left lateral chest, punched through the top of the left lung, skidded over the heart and the other lung and behind the aorta, exited through the right axilla, and re-entered the right arm, breaking the humerus and lodging in a bulge under the epidermis on the outside of the arm.

On the other hand, rifled slugs are famous for ending hostilities. Consider two famous, high volume gunfights.

Forensic researcher Alan Kulovitz took the famous autopsy photo of the Cook County, Illinois heroin addict who was shot 33 times with 9mm. Winchester 100-grain PowerPoint (softnose, non-hollowpoint) pistol bullets and remained on his feet, attempting to reload the .45 automatic he had emptied at the officers who were armed with Smith & Wesson model 59 pistols. As he bent over attempting the reload, one officer shot him in the back with a 12-ga. rifled slug. Because of the angle, it travelled through muscle only before entering the thoracic cavity above the lung and exited just below the collarbone. This large exit hole is visible in the autopsy photo, published in the widely-used police trailing manual "Street Survival." The officer fired again, and the second rifled slug shattered the spine and destroyed the heart, slowed enough by the heavy resistance of the vertebrae that it lodged spent, beneath the breastbone. At this point, the gunman finally collapsed and died.

In the mid-'80s Grand Concourse shootout in the Bronx, a crack junkie who had murdered a dealer and another doper then engaged a large number of officers in a protracted running gunfight. Hit a total of 18 times with .38 Special bullets, he was still running and attempting to reload his own .38 Special when an Emergency Services officer fired a single Winchester 12-ga. hollowpoint rifled slug into his torso, dropping him dead.

Despite the shotgun's massive power, then, we learn that the defender must be ready to instantly "inject another dose". A downed suspect can revive, and the effect of a first shot that appears to neutralize may only be temporary.

One of my police graduates entered a hostage scene with his Remington 870 at the ready, and when the suspect moved as if to stab the victim, shot him in the chest. The man jerked violently, stiffened upright, and ceased his assaultive behavior as if stunned. This gave a second SWAT officer time to grab the woman and jerk her away out of danger. A moment later, the suspect lunged at the first officer with a knife, and the latter fired a second shot. This time the suspect collapsed. Both rounds were 12-ga. Winchester hollowpoint rifled slugs; the second had shattered the spine. Amazingly, the suspect survived both wounds though paralyzed for life.

Terminal ballistics are learned only in flesh. Author has made a point of debriefing such men as Dr. Werner Weisenhoffer, head of cardiac surgery at the University of Vienna.

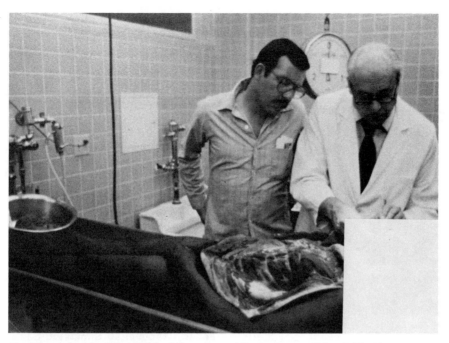

Dr. Joseph Davis, Chief Medical Examiner of Dade County (Miami) Florida.

Ron Flud, Chief Coroner of Clark County (Las Vegas) Nevada . . .

. . . and Col. Martin Fackler, MD, chief expert on wound ballistics at US Army's Letterman Hospital at The Presido.

Each shotgun will throw different buckshot loads in different patterns. These are typical for 7 yards and were fired from a cylinder-bore Benelli 12-gauge.

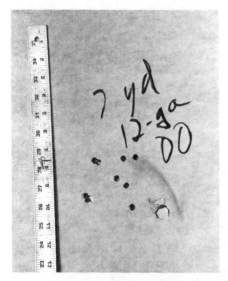

Standard 00 buckshot. 4" pattern is typical. 9 .33 cal. pellets.

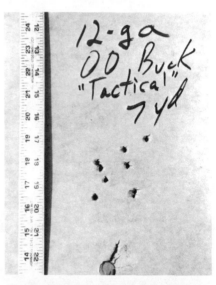

Federal Tactical 00 Buckshot. Same pattern size, less recoil. Also 9 .33 cal. pellets.

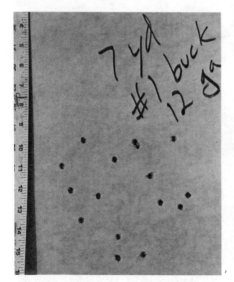

#1 buckshot. Pattern is 6", with significantly better saturation. Author's favorite. 16 .30 cal. projectiles.

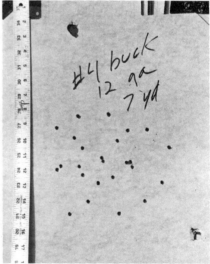

#4 buckshot. Pattern is 7". 27 pellets, each about .23 cal.

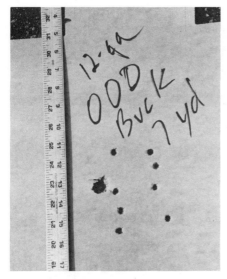

000 buckshot. Note unusual "box" pattern 8 .36 cal. projectiles in 5" group.

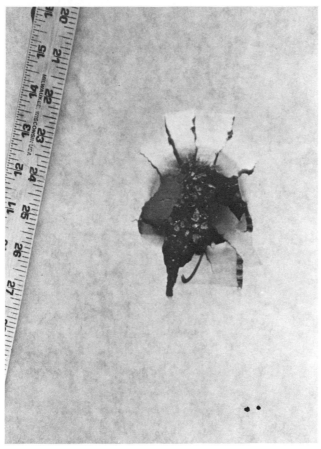

Correlate this muzzle contact "wound" on cardboard target with those seen in human flesh. Diameter of destroyed area is much larger than muzzle diameter. 00 buckshot shown, but any full load would do same at muzzle contact, in 12-ga.

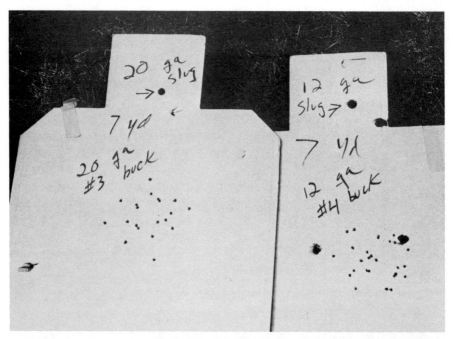

This is why author likes light-kicking 20-ga. for close range defense. Each target has been hit once in head with slug, once in chest with buckshot, 20-gauge on the left and 12-gauge on the right. 20-ga. #3 buck has 20 pellets, each .25 cal.; 12-ga. #4 buck has 27 pellets, each .23 cal. Medical examiner would be hard pressed to tell the difference, as would the "patient." Ragged holes here and in some other pictures are from shotshell wadding materials.

Then Deerfield (NH) Police Chief Paul Dewey demonstrates individual characteristics of shotgun patterns. Standard cruiser 20" 12 ga. with improved cylinder choke shot 00 buck into bottom pattern; 14" Stakeout gun shot same load into slightly larger pattern center, with cylinder choke; and 20-ga. 14" Stakeout shot top group with #3 buckshot. Note gap in latter pattern, and comparative pattern sizes. All three pump shotguns are Ithaca Model 37s.

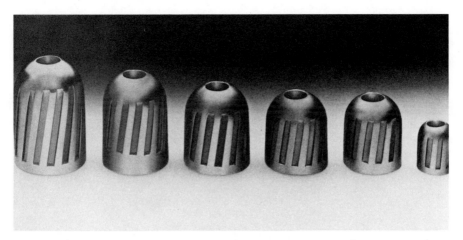

Hollowpointed Foster style rifled slugs by Federal, in sizes from 10 gauge (far left) to .410 bore (far right). Photo courtesy Federal Cartridge.

3" Magnum load of 000 buckshot gives only ten .36 caliber pellets to the eight of a standard load, with much moe recoil; relative combat efficiency is reduced with this heavy round. Photo courtesy Federal Cartridge.

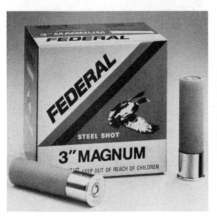

Steel shot, lighter and less penetrative than lead, may be of interest to those whose mission requires very limited penetration at very close range. This is 3" Magnum 20-gauge #6 size birdshot, from Federal. Photo courtesy Federal Cartridge.

Designed to give better long range performance to hunters, copper-plated 00 short Magnum load (Federal 12-gauge) may be overpenetrative for close-range antipersonnel use. Photo courtsey Federal Cartridge.

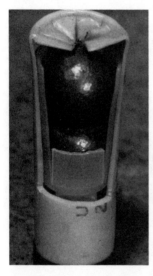

Twin .570 musket balls handloaded into a 20-gaug shell have more raw impact and are more penetrative than #3 buckshot, but will have less saturation effect in flesh. Load is fine for combat/pin matches, but unproven in human combat. Photo courtesy Jim Burnett.

Because a wide range of defensive loads exists only in 12-gauge, shotgun owners more than handgun owners have good reason to handload their own "duty ammo." Photo courtesy Jim Burnett.

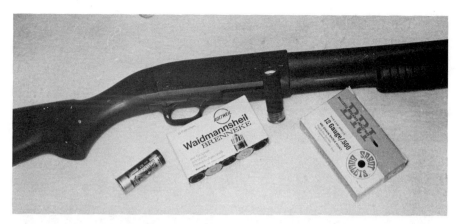

Brenneke slugs, left are superbly accurate but overpenetrative; same tends to be true of rocket shaped sabot slugs at right. Gun is Ithaca model 37 Police shotgun.

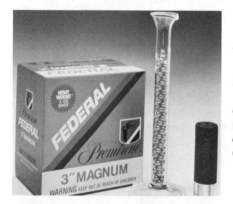

Those who insist on using birdshot for home defense or police raid/entry work should use #6 or BB size minimum; 3" Magnum 12 ga. Federal Premium shells carry two full ounces of shot, twice as much lead as a standard 00 12-gauge combat round. Photo courtesy Federal Cartridge.

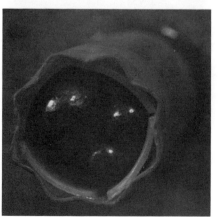

Mixed load of five large pellets and ten small ones should be deadly; British used a similar concept with 12-gauge Brownings in jungle warfare. This is 20-gauge shell handloaded by Jim Burnett.

Muzzle contact: At instant of shot, target is thrown backward away from Benelli. Note huge hole by muzzle blast; similar volume of damage may occur in soft tissue with muzzle contact.

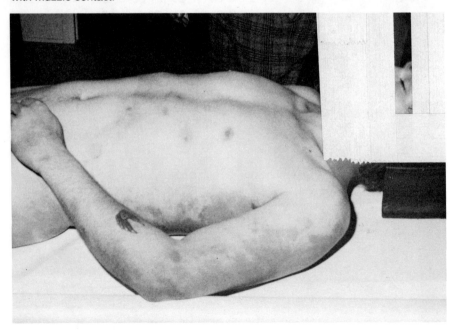

Subject appears to be sleeping, but death was not that tranquil. Note small circular blemishes on midsection.

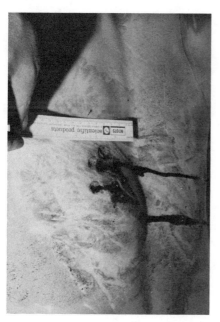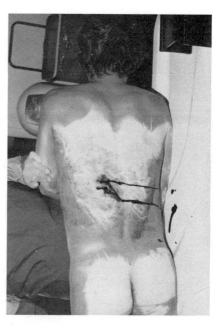

He was shot w/12-gauge as he attempted to kill a cop. Entry wound is in back; note livor mortis, indicating that he died in a supine position.

Close-up of entry shows nine .33 pellets patterned little more than two inches apart.

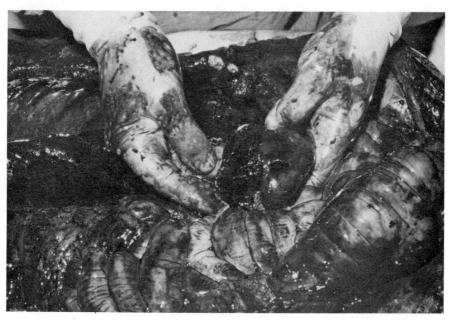

Saturation effect of multiple projectiles is clear as autopsy reveals massive extent of damage inside torso. See next page also.

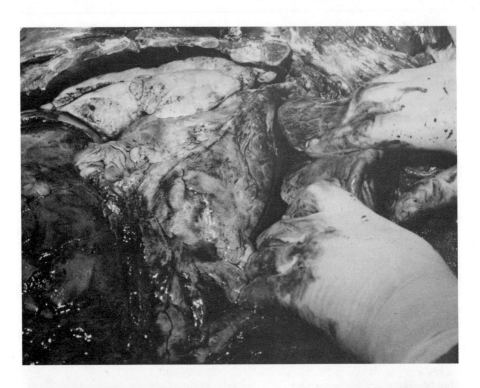

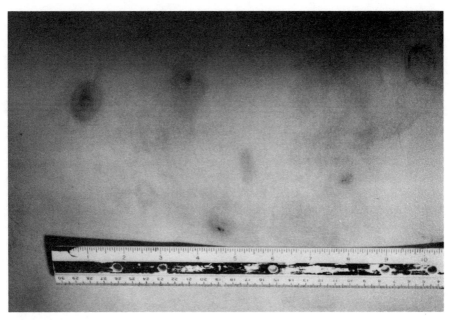

"Blemishes" are revealed to be bruising caused from inside out during last seconds of life as buckshot pellets stopped just under the stretchy epidermis before exiting chest. Note that "billiard ball effect," even without striking major bone, has tripled pellet spread to perhaps six inches. Failure of any pellets to exit was unusual, and due in part to the fact that deceased was a large man.

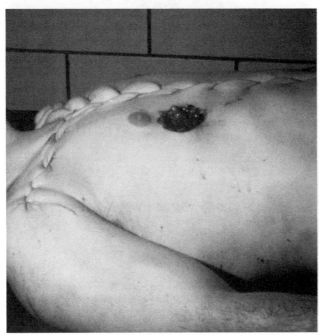

Instant death caused by muzzle contact blast of 12-ga. oo buck traversing chest right to left and front to back. Stippling is absent because gunshot residue was absorbed in heavy clothing. This is "tunnel wound" or "rat-hole wound" effect.

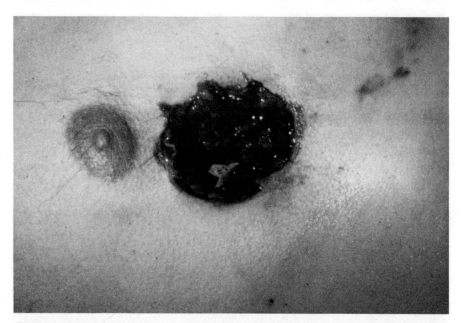

Close-up of wound in previous photo. Note that size of permanent cavity is much larger than bore diameter of shotgun. Compare this wound with photo elsewhere of muzzle-contact buckshot blast on cardboard target. Gases from shotgun muzzle blast contribute to the physical damage.

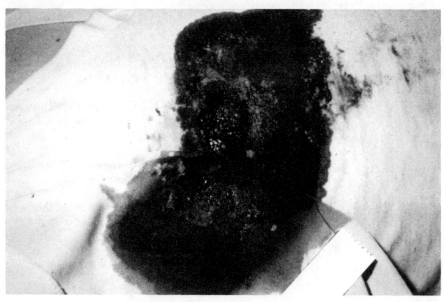

Prior to autopsy, clothing of this victim was peeled off and photographed *in situ*. Note that gunshot residue has been captured in layers of clothes. This is why in situ examination of clothes and preservation of same is critical to homicide investigation.

Deformed buckshot pellets removed from distal side of this victim's body. 00 buck is less likely to overpenetrate on widthway shots. Note that wadding was also recovered from corpse.

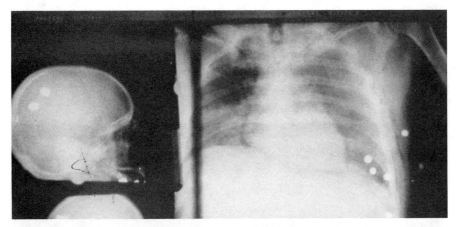

X-ray of same shooting victim shows "billiard ball effect" as pellets dispersed widely through tissue, even without striking heavy bone. Adjacent radiographs show subject was also shot twice in the head.

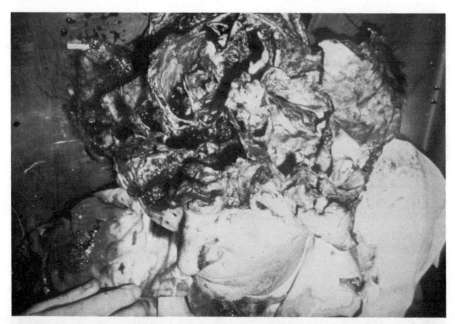

Muzzle contact shotgun wounds to the head are literally explosive. It takes some people a moment to realize this was once a human head; orient to nose, mouth, and chin at 6 o'clock more or less in place. This is the typical injury pattern of execution murder with 12-gauge shotgun muzzle touching victim's forehead.

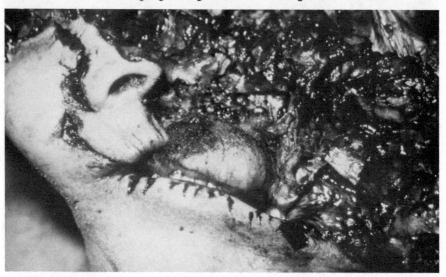

Intra-oral 12-gauge gunshot wound. Normally associated with suicide, this wound pattern also occurs in victims of psychosexually motivated criminals who make them suck the muzzle of the killer's gun before the trigger is pulled. Brain and eyes have been blown out, and skull literally exploded from within. Note multiple tears on resilient lower lip, due to stretching from massive gas blast creating back pressure in mouth.

28

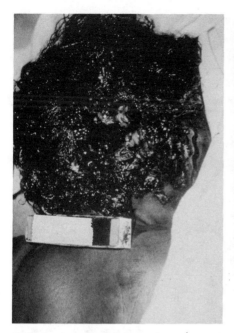

Entry wound of 00 buckshot (12-ga) shell from close range, within a few feet. Entering back of head, pellets have struck en masse creating a massive, shattered entry cavity. This was an execution murder.

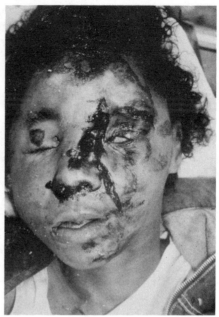

This is the exit area. Young woman's face shows "bloody mask effect," since maxillofacial structure has been smashed and skull has lost integrity of shape. Note billiard ball effect, and that fact that five of nine pellets have exited. This is the typical exit pattern with 00 buckshot at close range.

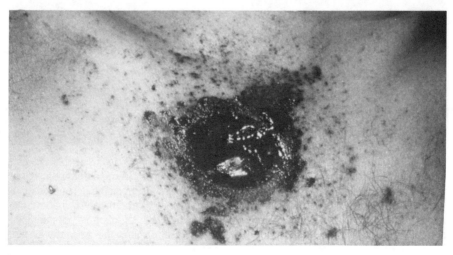

Note that tunnel wound effect occurs with 20-gauge as well as 12-gauge shotguns at muzzle contact distances.

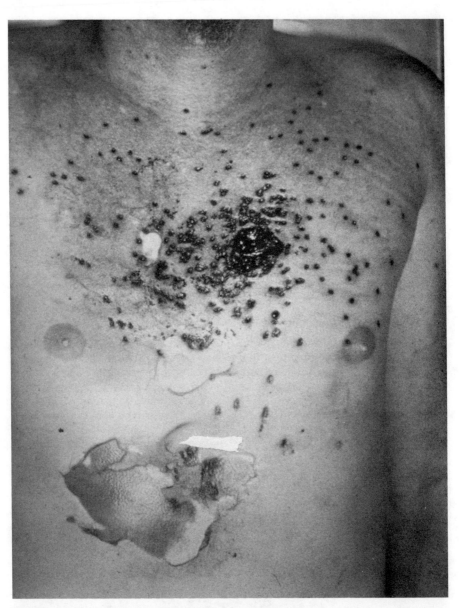

Multiple lessons are learned from this murder victim. He was shot twice with 12-ga. shotgun loaded with #6 birdshot. The first blast caught him as he stood at the back of a vehicle, the shot fired some 15 steps away. Birdshot pattern is distributed across the victim's chest. He fell on his back, and killer moved in, firing from near downed man's feet. This accounts for bevelling of second, tunnel wound just left of center chest. Most of charge has struck en masse, with some stray pellets around the epicenter of the wound joining in the saturation effect accomplished by the first round. Injury on abdomen is thermal burn from exhaust pipe of running automobile, near which this victim fell.

Chapter 4

Condition of Readiness

In combat shotgun parlance, "ready position" refers to the user's stance when grasping a loaded weapon, while "condition of readiness" refers to the status of the gun vis-a-vis its ammo supply, that is, its mechanical readiness to fire.

Different experts define different conditions of readiness. The terms used at Lethal Force Institute for StressFire shotgun training are easily understood, and are as follows.

UNLOADED. There are no cartridges in the gun, either in the magazine or in the chamber(s).

UNLOADED AND READY. This distinction is made for the benefit of civilian students, who have to worry about laws that do not affect serving police officers. In some states – Missouri, for example – a gun immediately adjacent to cartridges that will fire in it is considered "in a state of readiness" and treated in a manner not unlike a loaded gun in the eyes of the law. An Unloaded and Ready gun would be a shotgun with no cartridges inside the mechanism (magazine or chambers) but with shells attached to the gun in a butt cuff, Speed-Feed stock,etc. While considered unloaded from a range safety point of view, such a weapon would be considered in a condition of readiness and illegal for a civilian to have in his car in that manner in a state such as Missouri.

CRUISER READY. In this status, the firing chamber is empty but the magazine is loaded with X number of cartridges. The gun will be made ready to fire by chambering a round and proceeding accordingly.

By definition, a breech-loading gun like a double barrel or single-shot shotgun has no magazine and cannot be loaded cruiser ready. Naturally, if any gun has so much as one cartridge anywhere inside its mechanism, it is seen in the eyes of the law as a loaded firearm.

For practical reasons, savvy shotgunners load their magazines to one less shell than full capacity in cruiser ready, sometimes two shells down with extended magazines. Thus, a standard Remington 870 with a 5-shot capacity (4-shell magazine plus chambered round) becomes a 3-shot weapon when actually loaded to cruiser ready. This is another advantage of extended magazine shotguns. A seven-plus-one capacity shotgun will, in cruiser ready, have an empty chamber and six shells in the magazine, double the capacity of a similarly carried gun of only four-plus-one capacity.

LOADED AND CHAMBERED or LOADED AND READY. In this condition, the gun's magazine is at least partially loaded, and *there is a shell in the firing chamber.* This condition is distinct from "fully loaded" in that the gun will typically have begun in cruiser ready and had a round chambered from the magazine, and absent spare shells from a source outside the mechanism itself, the gun cannot by definition be loaded to full capacity. If time permits, the user would be wise to "top off" the weapon to full capacity before proceeding further.

Some recommend that when the shotgun is deployed with the possibility of facing a dangerous criminal the chamber be left empty, to reduce the likelihood of an accidental discharge and to allow the officer to "create the psychological advantage of racking the shotgun to chamber a round, a sound known to terrify criminals."

Let us pause to analyze this. The author is aware of documented cases of felony suspects "freezing like rabbits" at the sound of a shotgun being pumped. However, he is equally aware of numerous cases in which felony suspects were bluffed into submission at the point of an empty gun. The author respectfully submits that neither is the sort of dynamic you want to trust your life to.

Yes, the sound of the shotgun being charged may freeze the bad guy in his tracks.

However, if the offender is a streetwise, hardened criminal, the sound of you chambering the shell at the last instant may send him another message. *It may tell him that he is up against someone so incredibly stupid that he just now realized it might be a good idea to have a loaded gun in his hand, a gun he could fire a shot with. It tells him that you were sufficiently slow to react to danger, that up until now, you were facing him with a gun you could not immediately fire.*

This can negate deterrence. This can tell the offender something he wants to believe: that you can be taken. It can turn what might have been his bloodless surrender into his attempt to murder you, and whether he succeeds or whether you kill him instead – and the two outcomes are not mutually exclusive – leaving your gun with an empty chamber when you prepared to confront what you had reason to believe was a dangerous felon has forced you down from a win-win situation to a lose-lose situation.

The author respectfully suggests that any situation that warrants you breaking out a shotgun, warrants a round in the chamber immediately. Having lost count of the times I have deployed a shotgun on police duty, I can tell you that every single time, a shell went into the chamber as soon as the gun was in my hands.

The gun then went "on safe." *It is imperative to prevent a premature or accidental discharge that the loaded and chambered or loaded and ready shotgun be on safe during movement and approach, and depending on the situation, perhaps even when the suspect is at gunpoint. The finger or thumb should be on the safety, ready to instantly off-safe the gun and fire.*

Having led a relatively sheltered life, the author has taken about five people at gunpoint with shotguns. In all cases, a round was chambered. Each time, the weapon was a 12-gauge pump, department-issue Ithaca or Winchester, and in three of those cases the situation had progressed to the point where it was necessary to remove the safety and place the finger on the trigger. In two of those cases, the finger was actually applying pressure at the moment one suspect dropped his .22 caliber semiautomatic pistol, and the other ceased to reach for the handgun he pretended to be armed with.

In the latter two cases, there was no time to play with. If the gun had had to be pumped to fire at the final moment, time that was used in the judgment process would have had to be spent on operating the mechanism of the gun, and the shot would have had to be fired. The author would have wound up killing two men whom instead he was able to take into custody without bloodshed because the shotgun was already loaded and chambered when the confrontations began.

FULLY LOADED. The shell has been chambered from cruiser ready, and the officer has had time to access spare ammo from glove box, belt, carrier attached to the weapon, or whatever. The gun is now at its full stated shell capacity. It should still be "on safe" until the need to fire has made itself clear. All comments from LOADED AND READY or LOADED AND CHAMBERED apply.

Why Cruiser Ready?

This book recommends that the loaded shotgun in storage be kept in cruiser ready condition, whether it is in fact in a police cruiser or is kept for immediate security in a private home. The reason is that no shotgun currently produced, to the author's knowledge, has a firing pin safety, and if there is a shell in the chamber and a drop or fall causes the gun to strike a hard surface in a certain way, *the chambered shell can discharge even if the safety catch is "on" and the trigger has not been touched.* This movement of the firing pin inside its channel is known as an "inertia fire" and is well known to court-certified expert witnesses who have to testify in the wake of tragic accidental shooting incidents.

Another good reason is that there is always the possibility that an offender will get his hands on your weapon before you do. This could happen if you are a householder who arrives home while the burglary is in progress and the burglars already have their hands on your shotgun, or if you are a police officer attacked during a traffic stop and an accomplice of the person you are fighting gets into your cruiser and figures out how to operate the lock that holds your shotgun to the dashboard of the cruiser.

There are two schools of thought on fine points of cruiser ready.

One theory is that the gun should have a loaded magazine and empty chamber and be off-safe, hammer down so the slide can be pumped and a shot fired instantly. The theory is that under stress your brains will turn to crap, you won't remember the location of the safety catch or the slide release, and you will be unable to fire to protect your life. "Pump the gun, pull the trigger" is supposedly all you'll be able to manage.

The other theory is that the gun should have loaded magazine and empty chamber and be cocked and *on* safe, requiring anyone who wants to shoot the gun to depress the slide release, operate the slide, and release the safety catch before the gun can be fired. This can be done in perhaps one second by a trained and practiced individual. The theory is that if an unauthorized person gets hold of your shotgun, anyone who watches television knows enough to pump the front end and pull the trigger but only someone familiar with the gun can accomplish the "manual of arms" that releases both the slide lock and the trigger-locking manual safety.

The author goes with the latter view. The shotgun is not an instant reaction weapon like the constantly carried pistol, and as generations of auto pistol carriers have shown it can become second nature to release a firearm's safety as you draw to fire. The same works very well with the shotgun. No, it won't work if you don't know the gun, but if you don't know the gun you don't have any business messing with something as deadly as a shotgun, *do* you?

The feeling here is that someone too stupid to know how to operate their shotgun is very probably too stupid to be entrusted with one to begin with. The added safety margin given to "on safe" storage of pump or auto shotgun, plus a pump shotgun locked on an empty chamber, can go far toward preventing a tragedy if the gun enters the hands of unauthorized persons. For the trained user, the penalty enacted in reaction time is virtually nil.

Chapter 5

Ready Positions

There are numerous "ready stances" for use with the combat shotgun. In a combat match, the range supervisors will tell you what stances to use, and their advice should of course be followed. For danger situations, however, the following suggestions are offered.

LOW READY. Sometimes called "Rhodesian ready," this is actually an old hunter's technique in which the butt of the gun is placed in the shoulder pocket, the shooter is almost in a firing stance, and the muzzle is depressed just below line of sight for clear view of the target area. A simple lift of the forward hand brings the gun to bear on the target. It is very quick; however, because the weight of the gun is borne almost entirely by the extended forward arm, it is also quickly fatiguing.

Hunters in the woods, and the Rhodesian Army in the field, correctly anticipated a confrontation that would take place at some distance, and did not have to worry about being attacked by a felon who intended to disarm them. A shotgun in Low Ready is the most difficult to defend against a deflection or disarm, and similarly, is the easiest gun for someone else to deflect, or to take away from the legitimate user.

Suitable for matches or situations where the encounter can be predicted to take place at a distance, a Low Ready is among the worst choices for a building or house search. In addition to the weapon retention problem, the gun muzzle is level with furniture and will bump as the officer moves in the dark. This can trigger a predictable startle reflex that can cause the officer's finger to close, firing a shot. At best, it alerts the criminals he's looking for to his presence; at worst, that shot could injure another officer or blow the cop's own foot off.

The one time a Low Ready would make sense during a building search would be when descending a ramp or a flight of stairs; with nothing in the way to snag the gun, and the way clear to scan for suspects who might grab the gun, it is now safe to take advantage of the fact that the Low Ready position would give almost instant acquisition of a hostile target emerging below.

TACTICAL HIGH READY. Such master shotgun competitors as John Satterwhite have proven that the International Skeet Ready position is extremely fast for mounting the gun. It turns out also to be the strongest position in which to resist a disarming attempt from virtually any angle. So long as you look past the weapon instead of holding at eye level, it will not obscure your "danger scan."

You will want to have only the muzzle and the front sight in view. When these come into line with the opponent, the gun is pushed forward and the butt then brought back into the shoulder – all in line with the target – for an extremely efficient and swift alignment of gun with opponent. The gun is pushed forward first to prevent the gun butt snagging on heavy clothing at the shoulder. This is particularly likely to occur with the tacky surface of a recoil pad coming against a nylon or leather police jacket; wise old street cops like to round off the top edges of the recoil pads on their shotguns for just this reason.

ONE HAND READY. One handed low ready makes no sense at all. One handed high ready can, if necessary, leave a hand free for vital tasks. The gun can be quickly brought to bear.

Perhaps even faster is a one-handed hold in which the muzzle is level with the anticipated target's position. If necessary, a hit can be delivered one-handed. Tucking the butt of the gun into the arm with the comb of the stock under the armpit will not only stabilize the weapon for the shot, but make your hold much stronger if you are suddenly attacked for the gun.

TWO-HAND LEVEL READY. Moving with the shotgun levelled straight in front of you, in a position like a High Tuck that does not obscure your view, allows swift reaction and puts you in a very stable position in which to defend against a disarm attempt. However, the gun muzzle is now probing well out ahead of your body. For this reason, it should not be used when approaching a hiding place where someone could quickly grab it, or where its extended silhouette could give your position away prematurely.

CRADLE CARRY. Widely taught in hunter safety programs, the cradle carry can be dangerous if the officer lets the muzzle get too low, at which time it will be pointed at those to his side who are not immediately in his field of view. The cradle carry works very effectively, however, if the gun muzzle is kept on a high angle.

Cradle carry should be done WITH BOTH HANDS, not just with the gun in the weak arm! With the gun hand on the pistol grip, the cradling weak arm creates perhaps the most strongly defensible hold against a gun grab, and the gun can be mounted to fire with amazing swiftness. Since the arms are flexed and the gun is toward the lower center of the body – bringing the gun's center of balance toward the body's center of gravity – it is perhaps the least fatiguing of ready positions. This can serve you well in an all-night manhunt, as the author discovered in that situation some time ago.

HIGH PROFILE READY. Probably better suited for administrative handling or management of the gun in non-risk situations, this stance places the butt of the gun on the edge of the hip or the belt, the muzzle up, and the firing hand in control of the pistol grip of the weapon. One is vulnerable to attack from the flank by a disarmer in this position (the response would be to pivot away, bringing the elbow back to line the muzzle up with the assailant), and it should be used only in safe areas during a break in the manhunt or whatever. It is extremely useful on the training range.

POSITIONS TO AVOID. Carrying the gun *over the shoulder*, as has been recommended in some hunter safety programs, is dangerous for a number of reasons. Your body will instinctively want to roll the gun off the collarbone and onto the cushioning muscle, which puts the gun muzzle horizontal and pointed at anyone behind you. It is also almost impossible to defend against a disarming attempt from behind.

So-called *low profile carries* seem good in theory but work poorly in field practice. In this hold, the muzzle is up, the barrel along the upper arm, with the hand down at the side and cupping the trigger guard/rear receiver area. This is one of the weakest positions from which to defend against a weapon snatch, is not terrible secure against even dropping the gun, and will not be as fast to react as a conventional high or low ready.

Another low profile method currently in vogue is holding the gun in the dominant hand only, muzzle down, at the side and slightly away from the body. The gun can be lost just to bumping on an object when walking, let alone an aggressive disarm attempt, and will be slow to bring to bear if needed; in snow or mud, the muzzle can become plugged, causing the barrel to explode if fired. The author recommends strongly that this technique not be used.

When an instructor is asked, "What is the purpose of our low-profile technique to begin with?", the response is usually, "So it won't alarm or upset people when they see the shotgun."

Let us stop and think about this for a moment. When the situation is sufficiently dangerous for you to be walking around with a shotgun in view, noncombatants damn well *better* be alarmed and upset, hopefully sufficiently so to get out of the way. If the presence of the shotgun, and not the situation that warranted its presence, is what upsets them, they are in need of a serious "reality check." Even if the gun brings complaints, it will bring them irrespective of whether the gun is in high ready or low ready; the only thing that will make it worse is pointing the gun at them, which you won't do to bystanders anyway.

Going to a low profile position makes you appear to be hiding the shotgun. It gives the body language of shame and embarrassment, and creates the impression that you yourself think you have overreacted or overstepped your bounds by deploying the shotgun in the first place.

Just an an inherently lethal weapon should never be used in an attempt to inflict non-lethal injuries, an inherently high profile weapon can never effectively be turned into a low profile one. The author would respectfully suggest that any "low profile carry" be put far in the back of the closet in your repertoire of combat shotgun techniques.

High ready, sometimes called port arms, is the preferred technique of those who shoot both clay birds and feathered ones. Author feels it also makes excellent sense for close quarters defense work, since a shotgunner is already habituated to it, it's very quick, and as shown elsewhere it gives shooter an advantage in a weapon retention situation.

Low ready, known by different names, is the most commonly recommended ready position for combat shotgun, and author's second favorite. It can be quickly fatiguing and reduces weapon retention capability, but is quite fast. Author would use low ready while defending a static position, high ready while tactically moving during a search.

One-hand ready. Buttstock is in armtuck, firing hand gripping gun firmly when free hand is required for doorknob, radio, etc. This gives maximum speed of response whether defensive gunfire or weapon retention should suddenly be called for, and is extremely secure.

Known among some police as "hi-profile carry," this position with butt resting on hip gives quick access and eliminates fatigue when long gun must be constantly ready in a "reasonably secure" area, such as outer perimeter of siege or manhunt. Not for imminent combat, however, due to slightly slowed response and particularly, limitation on weapon retention capability.

Not recommended! This common shoulder carry tends to wind up with gun pointing straight backward at another good guy behind you. Speed is not optimal, and weapon retention capability is poor.

Not recommended! Over-forearm carry is slow, offers limited retention capability, and tends to cause gun to point at those ahead of you unintentionally.

Though recommended by some for "low profile" carry, this is Not Recommended by LFI! Gun muzzle can easily become plugged; it is perhaps the single weakest hold in terms of retention; it is prone to accidental discharge; and it is very slow if gun is neded for its intended purpose.

Another widely recom- mended carry position, this form of the "low profile" technique offers poor retention, is not as fast as it could be. Author would not use it in any remotely dangerous situation. Its only application to him is while standing on the range listening to a lecture from an instructor, and even then, Hi- profile carry might be better.

"Cradle carry" allc surprisingly fast respor and gives very g protection against disa attempts. It is comfortable long-term carry such extended manhunts. careful, however, that mu: does not point toward par on that side. Demonstra these ready positions Mitchell Rosen.

42

Chapter 6

Selecting Action Types

A shotgun's "action type" refers to the manner of its operating mechanism. The primary shotguns in use today for combat purposes are magazine fed, and either semiautomatic or pump action.

The *semiautomatic shotgun* utilizes either the gases generated by burning gunpowder, or the raw recoil force of the shot going off, to cycle the mechanism — that is, to eject the spent shell casing that was just fired and rechamber another fresh shell ready for another immediate shot. Whether gas-operated or recoil-operated, this design is called "autoloading" or "semiautomatic" because while the next shell is brought into position automatically, the shot has to be fired by an intentional pull of the trigger each time. This is distinct from an "automatic" weapon like a machinegun in which one pull of the trigger keeps many rounds firing until trigger pressure is released. The term "automatic shotgun" is colloquially used for semiautomatic shotguns but is generally considered to be semantically incorrect.

The *pump action or slide action shotgun*, known colloquially as a "pump gun," is similar to a semiautomatic in appearance but the forward handle or "fore-end" is actually a sliding piece known as a slide handle, slide, or pump. After a shot is fired, the gun cannot fire again until this handle is pulled sharply back all the way, then snapped all the way forward again. The rearward movement ejects the fired shell and cocks the hammer, and allows another fresh round to come from the magazine onto a shell lift or lifter; the forward stroke brings this shell into the firing chamber so the gun may be shot once more. In effect, the forward hand is doing what the internal mechanism of an autoloader's action does.

These are the two shotgun types used by serious combat shooters, police, and soldiers. Other types of shotgun are available, but are generally unsuited for combat work. They include the following.

Single-shot shotguns can fire only one shot at a time, and do not have a *magazine*, or reservoir of additional shots. Since an estimated 40% of armed encounters involve more than one armed opponent, a single-shot weapon leaves the user doomed from the start nearly half the time. In addition, one of the best-trained American police departments reports hits with only 58% of all shots fired with their shotguns in action, further reducing the survival potential of some armed with a one-shot weapon.

Double barrel shotguns have separate firing chambers for two shotgun shells, fired by separate mechanisms that may be connected to a separate trigger or activated by twin triggers. Only two shots at once can be fired. Generally considered reliable, "doubles" have been obsolete for gunfighting purposes since the advent of the slide action shotgun in the 1890's. The double barrel is often recommended for home defense.

This is because it can give the instant choice of two different types of cartridge, i.e., a multi-projectile "shot load" such as a few heavy buckshot pellets or up to hundreds of tiny birdshot pellets, or a massive one-ounce rifled slug measuring nearly three-quarters of an inch in diameter and travelling 1400 feet per second. Another reason is that its hinged-rear, "breech loading" design is simple, and the theory is that people new to guns need the simplest possible equipment.

Unfortunately, the use of deadly weapons against violent offenders is not a simple matter. I once came under the command of a new chief of police who had been an NYPD detective, perhaps the only class of American law enforcement still using double barrel shotguns (the discontinued Stevens model 311). He wanted to trade the department's 12-gauge cruiser pump guns for double barrels. Rather impolitically, I explained that two-shot guns for defense only made sense when issued to people with two-digit IQ's, and that while NYPD might insult its detectives' intelligence by issuing them guns for the stated reason that they were "idiot proof," I did not feel my brother patrolmen warranted the same insult. Though I would pay for that statement — the chief of police in question hates my guts to this day — I would never apologize for it. Obsolete for combat for a century, the double barrel's only place today is in sport-

44

shooting, where its balance makes it excel, or in the situation of an armed citizen who happens to own one and can't afford to buy a more efficient defense weapon yet.

Bolt Action shotguns are cheap to produce and are therefore plentifully available. Their stock shapes are often such that they magnify recoil; a four-step movement to chamber a fresh shell also takes the firing hand away from the trigger and makes bolt guns pathetically slow to recycle when a second shot is required; and they have never been used intensively enough by anyone serious about it to see if their low-budget construction would stand up under the pounding of the heavy training that should be mandatory for anyone presuming to wield so powerful and deadly a weapon as the combat shotgun. No serious expert would condone, let alone recommend, the bolt action's shotgun's use for combat.

Pump Versus Auto

The semiautomatic (autoloading, or "auto") shotgun and the pump gun are the two primary contenders in the combat shotgun field. Each have their advocates, equally well credentialed. Such experts as Lewis Awerbuck and John Farnam are on record as preferring the slide action, while the equally impressive Jeff Cooper and Ray Chapman just as strongly favor the autoloader. Competitive shooters — champions such as John Shaw and John Satterwhite — go almost 100% with the autoloader for gunfight-simulating "action shooting matches."

Slide action advantages are numerous. Chief among them is cost effectiveness: a pump costs only 75% as much as an autoloader of equivalent quality. The very popular Remington brand starts its model 870 pump gun at 75% of the price of its 11-87 autoloader. Cost is the primary reason why police and military agencies, buying on bid, have standardized on the pump gun for routine as opposed to special-purpose users.

The slide action, because it is manually operated, also has the advantage of working better when dirty, rusty, improperly lubricated, fed with bad shells, or otherwise neglected. Its manual action allows its user to overcome, by main physical force, friction binds that would cause a semiautomatic to be jammed.

Due to the nature of its design, the pump action's parts do not have to extend back into the stock as do the mechanisms of most semiautomatic shotguns. This allows the pump gun to be modified into pistol grip or folding stock configuration far more easily than the semiautomatic shotgun. At this writing, virtually all pump guns are available in, or can be retrofitted to, super-compact pistol grip or folding stock formats. Only one autoloader, the expensive Sage

International conversion of the Remington 1100 by John Klein, can be so modified, and that on a strictly custom basis.

Because the pump gun works off human energy instead of energy exerted by the shotgun shell that was just fired, the slide action can handle all manner of very light to very heavy recoil shells, some of special purpose design, without the mechanism jamming due to the sort of changes in cartridge pressure curves that can affect a semiautomatic's cyclic rate.

Slide action disadvantages are seen mostly to the person new to the gun. The "old gunny" who has made pumping the action second nature will be less affected by the fact that a sharp forward-back movement is required for each shot, slowing down the rapid fire process. The fixed-breech design of the pump gun transmits maximum recoil force to the shooter's shoulder, unlike the kick-cushioning effect of the gas-operated autoloader, which bleeds off force from each shot fired to operate the mechanism. Also, the slide cannot be effectively worked from awkward positions, such as prone, or kneeling with the forward elbow on the forward knee.

Let us compare these factors with *semiautomatic disadvantages.* Having less raw mechanical force behind each stroke of the mechanism, an autoloader is more dependent on being kept clean and fed good cartridges, and concomitantly more vulnerable to jamming when fed rough or dirty shells or fired when the inside parts have dirt, carbon, and grit built up in them. This is a pump gun advantage for those who will store their weapons unattended without maintenance.

Many semiautomatic shotguns are regulated internally to work with a certain power level of shell, and are therefore limited in ammunition selection. This is not true of the manually-operated pump gun. Even the best of autoloading shotguns will not cycle with low-pressure rounds like "bird bombs" which fire a delayed-detonation charge in midair like firecrackers, or AAI Ferret tear-gas shells. Pump guns handle such special-purpose cartridges without a hitch.

Finally, the greater cost of the semiautomatic can be an impediment; a pump gun, now, beats an auto, on layaway. In some circumstances, two pump guns stored in strategic locations can be a more sensible plan than a single autoloader that may not always be accessible. The latter would be a factor in, say, retail store security, or the case of the homeowner who might want one weapon in the bedroom and another in the home office where he or she works late.

Autoloader advantages, however, are significant. With the gas-operated designs, reduced recoil allows quicker development of unhesitating high-speed shooting performance, especially on multiple targets. The human error-induced short stroke, an epidemic cause of pump shotgun malfunctions, is eliminated entirely. The student does not need to learn the complex psychomotor skill of operating a slide while simultaneously trying to control a muzzle and trigger, and in the author's opinion, there is sufficient saving of training time, training cost, and ammo expense to pay for the more costly semiautomatic in the long run.

Combat competition (as opposed to trap and skeet shooting) has taught us that the auto will dramatically outperform the pump. It has been many years since a major combat match was won by a pump against autos. As this book went to press, the proprietors of the Second Chance Street Combat Nationals had announced that shooters with pump guns would be given a one-second time bonus per run against those with autoloaders. Word from the competitors was that they would stay with their "automatics": a one-second head start wasn't enough to equal the odds. If this is the feeling among master shooters skilled with pump guns, one can easily deduce where it leaves the beginner.

In training street cops, the author in 1984 switched his police department from the Ithaca model 37, one of the smoothest pump shotguns, to the Benelli M1 121 semiautomatic. With the pump, the department had barely been able to achieve the required 70% minimum score on the easiest possible course. With the automatic, average scores went into the 90th percentile on the *toughest* available course: a quantum leap, indeed. The author's current department recently changed from the regulation Remington 870 pump to the Benelli Super 90 as a cruiser shotgun, and qualifications and confidence both leapt upward, averaging nearly 100%. The average shooter, police or civilian, will benefit from the switch from pump to auto much more dramatically than will the gun expert or experienced pump gun user.

A strong point in favor of the auto is that pumping a shotgun is a conditioned response that requires a large number of repetitions to become reflexive. In both field encounters and training, it is not uncommon to see the stressed-out shooter fire and fail to cycle the slide for a subsequent shot. The autoloader's design eliminates this potentially lethal hazard.

Virtually every pump gun manufacturer produces an autoloader; as a rule, you will find their autoloader more efficient for high-stress use than their pump gun.

The author's recommendation is the semiautomatic, unless cost is prohibitive. In that case, the reader will find that a used semiautomatic is often available at the local gunshop for the price of a new pump gun. Alternatively, one can buy the pump gun now, and save up to trade in on a suitable autoloader at a later time.

47

NYPD detectives prepare to qualify with their issue shotgun, the Stevens 311 12-ga. double barrel, at outdoor range on Rodman's Neck. Note mandatory ear and eye protection. Author took this photo in early '70s, but this gun is issue for NYC detectives at time of this book's publication.

Double barrel shotgun is more compact than other designs. Note this one, with shortened barrel and buttstock, in comparison with CZ Skorpion 7.65 mm. machine pistol and Colt .45 autoloading pistol.

Since the turn of the century, the pump shotgun has been the standard for law enforcement. Only in the late '80s and early '90s did manufacturers aggressively push the autoloader to the police market, as in this ad for the Remington 11-87 in *Law and Order* magazine.

Chapter 7

Alternatives to the 12-Gauge for Combat

The twelve gauge has always been the standard combat shotgun. Many leading experts scoff at any other choice. Why is the 12-gauge predominant?

"It always has been, that's why." Momentum. Inertia. Tradition. Certainly, the round is well-proven as a fight stopper within its range, and conservative cops hate to go from things they have lots of experience with, to things that they don't; this is why it took them so long to forsake traditional service revolvers for more efficient semiautomatic pistols.

Besides, the dual worlds of guns and law enforcement have both long been infused with the John Wayne Syndrome. One must be strong and manly, unafraid of any animal or person or gun. If the gun kicks brutally, why, it's that much more macho.

At the other end of the spectrum, one gun company marketed a .410 pump shotgun for women, suggesting it be loaded with birdshot for home defense. It will be noted that hunters consider .410 shotguns with *any* load to be inhumanely weak for use on small deer; these .410 users suggest the tiny shotgun be limited to squirrels and rabbits at fairly close range. The use of a squirrel gun against a 250-pound, rage-maddened speed freak thus blatantly defies common sense.

Much more practical is the 20-gauge shotgun. Delivering roughly the ballistic force of two .44 Magnum revolver rounds at once, the twenty is described by most shooters as having about half or little more than half the recoil of a 12-gauge loaded with the same type of projectiles. Throwing its lead at about the same velocity as a twelve, the twenty merely has less lead to throw. Typical payload in the 20-gauge shell is five-eighths of an ounce of lead, compared to a full ounce in the 12-gauge, assuming both are standard 2 3/4" shells.

A 5-pellet 00 buck load was once produced for the 20, but was dropped, probably because it was not efficient for the shell, giving it only 55% the payload of a 9-pellet 12-gauge, where by weight the twenty should deliver at least 62% as much lead as the bigger shell. This was because the large .33-cal. pellets did not efficiently stack to utilize the airspace inside the shell. Makers have standardized on #3 buckshot for the twenty. This delivers 20 pellets, each .25 caliber. #3 is not factory-offered in 12-gauge, but it is readily compared to #4 buckshot, which consists of .23 caliber pellets packed 27 to the shell in a standard 12-bore load.

This ups the efficiency of the 20-gauge to a maximum level, giving it 74% as many pellets of roughly equal size as the 12-gauge #4. The photos will show that remarkably similar saturation and wound patterns occur at range of 20 to 25 feet. It is safe to say the aggressive felon hit with either would be unlikely to know the difference. 75% as much lead for only 50% to 60% of the recoil is a favorable bargain.

When we recognize how much the lighter recoil improves performance against multiple targets, the twenty becomes even more advantageous. The writer has discovered that the beginning-to-average shotgunner will shoot *much* faster with the light-kicking 20 than with the twelve, generally hitting three targets with the smaller gun in the time it takes to hit two with the larger. Mathematically, if one accepts that .23-caliber #4 buck and .25-caliber #3 buck pellets are effectively equal, the three 20-ga. #3 shells place sixty projectiles on target in the same time two 12-ga. #4 shells deliver 54 pellets to two targets. The twenty has now put 10% more lead where it needs to be than did the twelve — *and, far more tactically important, allows the shooter to hit 50% more targets with the twenty than with the twelve.*

It is not merely a matter of numbers. It is a matter of survival. Let us say the given defender faces three armed, aggressive criminals. They ignore the homeowner's challenge and go for their guns. Assume it will take each of them two seconds to draw their pistols, aim, and deliver a fatal shot.

If the homeowner, typically, can only shoot two of them in less than two seconds with the larger shotgun, the third criminal will shoot and kill the defender. If in the same time of just under two seconds the homeowner can shoot each of them center with a twenty gauge, it is much less likely that the defender will take a bullet.

This ability — *of the new shooter to journeyman level shooter*—to fire half again as fast and take out half again as many multiple targets, is far more important than seven additional pellets in each wound channel. This combines with the light, fast handling of the typical 20-gauge shotgun. The Columbia, Missouri Police Department's Special Tactics and Response Team (STAR) adopted the 20-gauge 1100 as an entry gun because it handled like an ultralight .30 carbine when the officer had to pivot to unpredictable angles, and had all the stopping power these gunfight veterans felt they would ever need.

As the shooter becomes more skilled in controlling recoil, the gap in rapid-fire controllability between the small shotgun and the big one narrows. However, no matter how skilled one becomes with the big gun, one will always be faster with the smaller one. You, the reader, may be a better shot than the writer. You may be able to hit faster with a twelve than I can with a twenty. However, you will probably never be able to hit faster with a twelve than *you* can with a twenty.

If you have paid your dues and learned to hit with a 12-gauge as fast as you can pull the trigger, and the margin in speed between the twelve and the twenty is, for you, razor thin, certainly it makes sense *for you* to perhaps go to the twelve for the added power.

If you do not feel anything smaller than 000, 00, or #1 buckshot could ever be something that would give you confidence, the 12-gauge is your gun. If you anticipate raking shots on large, heavily clad offenders, it's a 12-gauge double-ought or triple-ought kind of night.

Remember, however, that very few of the people you share your training or advice with will ever be at the level you are, if in fact you can shoot a full-loaded twelve gauge with nearly the same speed and accuracy you can a twenty.

Indeed, if you have totally mastered recoil, it may be time for the 10-gauge Magnum. This monster 31/2"- long shell fires a payload equal to *two* standard twelve gauge shells at once. At the same velocity, it expels a two-ounce slug instead of a one ounce, eighteen double-ought pellets instead of nine, or 54 #4 pellets instead of 27. The only practical, proven combat guns for it at this writing are the Ithaca designed Mag-10, ideally in the short-barrel Roadblocker configuration, a weapon now produced by Remington, and the Browning BPS pump.

The gas system design is such that the magazine cannot be extended, limiting shell capacity to one in the chamber and two more in the magazine, merely a 50% increase in rounds over a double barrel, when working with the Mag-10.

Here we have a true specialty weapon. Weighing 101/2 pounds, it is awkward to react with when engaged by surprise from a flank. If, however, one had an unusual situation in which it was known beforehand that (a) there was only one opponent to deal with, and that (b) he would have to appear at a certain known place, and (c) there would be only time for one shot anyway with follow-ups impossible... in that situation, the author would reach for his Roadblocker.

It is difficult, however, to hypothesize such a police or self defense situation, which is doubtless one reason why the Roadblocker ten never found favor with police departments or armed citizens. The author *would* probably take it lion or leopard hunting were he inclined to stalk the great cats. A hard-learned practice among professional hunters in the African veldt is that when a wounded killer feline has gone into the bush and must be hunted down, a double-barrel 12-gauge with double-ought is the arm of choice, since the chance to fire will probably come as the well-concealed animal launches itself at you.

One does not see Roadblockers in the bush because most African nations prohibit hunting big game with semiautomatic weapons. However, it has also been noted that game rangers are easier and more reasonable to discuss things with than are great cats intent on turning you into sashimi.

Suffice to say that while the 20-gauge is a very useful combat option, one first recognized by iconoclastic gun expert Phil Engeldrum, the 10-gauge Magnum and the similar special-chambering 31/2" 12-gauge with a similar payload, are exotics that have very little place in actual self-defense work.

The 16-gauge shotgun, popular in Europe, is moribund in the US, with few loads and few guns available. Certainly, if one owns one of suitable design, it can be pressed into service with 4/5-ounce rifled slugs or a 12-pellet load of #1 buckshot.

The 28-gauge and .410 bore are altogether too feeble, in this writer's opinion, for home defense with shot loads. No mainstream-produce buckshot round exists for either at this writing, though three 000 pellets can be handloaded into a .410 shell. For perspective, however, Remington makes .38 Special revolver cartridges with *two* 000 buck pellets. No 28-gauge slug is presently produced, but the 1/5 ounce .410 slug — the only load in the caliber that can remotely be considered a predictable manstopper — is in a ballpark with the .44 Special revolver or .45 ACP (automatic Colt pistol) cartridge. Since a Marlin 8-shot .45 ACP semiautomatic carbine is available in the same price range as the .410 pump Mossberg markets for home defense, the Marlin Camp Carbine obsoletes the .410 for that purpose at the starting gate.

It is only fair for the author to list his own choices. Having paid my dues in learning the combat 12-bore, I generally use that shell size because (a) it's standard issue for my police department; (b) it's what most of my students show up with, so it's what I have to teach with; (c) my wife can handle my 12-gauge if she needs to, very effectively, but will probably go to a pistol anyway; and (d) there's a habit factor at work.

I will say this, however. If I remarried and my new wife was a petite female instead of the tall, strong, athletic woman I presently share my life with, the bedroom shotgun would be 20-gauge for commonality of confident useability. If I had not entered law enforcement where the twelve was standard, and if I'd known when much younger what I know now, I would have saved the time and punishment of mastering the big shotgun and started and stayed with the twenty gauge for home defense. Finally, as the hereditary arthritis inevitably creeps up on me, the passing years undoubtedly *will* find me a cranky old fart with a loaded twenty-gauge or two in the bedroom closet, and a collection of unloaded, cobwebbed 12-gauges kept in the gun cabinet for memories.

10-gauge Magnum delivers equivalent of two simultaneous blasts of 12-gauge at once. Ben Mozrall examines patterns of #4 buckshot, 54 pellets per shot. Photo courtesy *Law and Order* magazine.

Left to Right: Ithaca Roadblocker 10-ga. Magnum; Franchi SPAS-12 in 12-ga.; Remington LT-20 in 20 ga. All are semiautomatic. Weight of 20 is barely more than half that of either of the others.

Relative frame sizes are seen in 12-ga. (top) and 20-ga. Ithaca Stakeout shotguns.

Chapter 8

Brand Preferences

In teaching the combat shotgun at Lethal Force Institute, the author and his staff get to see a large number of guns of every type in heavy action. Some that work fine with light loads suffer problems with the constant battering of heavy combat ammo. Those that stand up the best, and have the best features for the stress-oriented techniques described in this book, are as follows.

Autoloaders

The BENELLI is probably the single most rugged autoloading shotgun on the market today. Reportedly, it was the first shotgun originally designed for the brutally demanding international military market instead of lightweight sporting use, although ironically its sporting version was the first to appear. In any case, it will be working reliably after the typical gas-operated shotgun has long since choked on carbon.

The first Benelli model (M1 121) required that the first shell be fed manually into the chamber. This makes it an excellent choice for those who prize a "proprietary nature to the user" factor that will make it quick and easy for the legitimate user to bring into action, but hard for an unauthorized, unfamiliar person to do the same. A retrofit was developed to allow a shell to be worked from the magazine, but its efficiency was spotty. When my department had the 121, we tried the retrofit and threw it away.

Benelli replaced the gun with the sleeker-looking Super 90, which also had better sights and a system that allowed a shell to be brought from the magazine into the chamber every time. The sights work better (no longer sending slugs low), a ghost ring sight and pistol grip assault stock are optional, and the older Benelli's reliability is not only maintained but enhanced. The old model didn't always work well with light, low-based birdshot; the Super 90 works with virtually everything but gas shells. It is available in 12-gauge only at this writing.

The BERETTA 1200 FP is made by the same people who produce the Benelli imported by HK. Handling qualities are similar. One sees, however, the occasional Beretta which will malfunction. This is generally found to be due to a weak magazine spring, which when replaced brings the gun up and running. 12 gauge only at this writing.

REMINGTON's 1100 in 12-gauge 2 3/4" length was designed for a lifetime of trap and skeet shooting, but tended to jam and break down when fired heavily with hot combat loads. Gunsmith Mike LaRocca pioneered the concept of altering the heavy duty 3" Magnum version to work with the shorter shells, solving the problem; Remington paid the ultimate compliment by going to the same concept with their current 11-87, which is a very reliable gas operated shotgun. These are the lightest kicking 12-gauge shotguns one can buy, along with the Winchester Super-X Model 1, also a heavy duty piece. The Winchester, however, has its safety on the front of the trigger guard, which LFI has found to be less desirable than the rear of the guard position seen on the Remington, Benelli, and Beretta.

In 20 gauge autos, Remington seems where it's at. The large-frame version can be made nearly recoil free, with the kick of a light carbine, while the 5 1/2 pound LT-20, with its slim English style stock and small frame, handles like a .22 rifle yet is still easily controllable in recoil. The 20-gauge shell does not beat up either size 1100 the way the 12-gauge did.

Slide Actions

In a 12-gauge pump, REMINGTON's classic 870 is hard to beat, so long as it has the FlexTab shell lift. Plain shell lifts can allow a shell to easily slip between lifter and bolt, causing the worst type of stoppage. This is even more epidemic with the 20-gauge 870 pumps.

MOSSBERG is not famous for glass-smooth actions, but their guns are light with good balance, and the natural top-tang safety catch makes sense. They are also low priced. For a period of years Mossberg quality control was unacceptably poor, but in recent years the model 500 and 590 have been showing good QC and reliability.

The Mossberg is probably the best buy in an economy-grade 12-gauge or 20-gauge pump. The ITHACA had better handling, though recent models have had rough quality control, a shame for a gun that was once the standard of the industry.

It should be noted that three styles of shotgun - most production runs of the Ithaca 37, and the older Winchester models 12 and 97 - could fire as the slide pumped if the trigger was merely held back. While some "gunshop commandoes" thought this was cool, the gun could not be effectively controlled in this fashion, and under stress it was entirely possible to accidentally discharge the gun while pumping the action.

There are many once-popular shotguns that are no longer made. The SMITH & WESSON 3000, made in Japan as sort of an improved Remington 870, was superb; S&W's older shotgun, the model 916 made on worn-out machinery bought from a B-grade gunmaker named Noble, was junk. Hi-Standard's 8113 was glass-smooth, but earned a reputation for parts breakage. The SPAS-12's gas system and 10 1/2 lb. weight soaked up recoil, but the gun had so many levers and switches it was practically crew-served, and it developed the nasty habit of going off when one released the safety catch.

To recap, the author would recommend the REMINGTON 1100 in a 20-gauge auto, and either the REMINGTON 11-87 (gas operated, light kick but will need more frequent cleaning) or BENELLI SUPER 90 (kicks harder but more maintenance free) in 12-gauge. If cost is no option the LAROCCA CUSTOM 1100 or 11-87 gives superior recoil control with excellent functioning.

In a pump, the author would recommend the REMINGTON 870 in 12-gauge but not 20, and the MOSSBERG 500 as first choice in 20-gauge and second choice in 12.

The reader is cautioned to avoid exotic weaponry. The drum-magazine 12-gauge Street Sweeper, the subject of numerous gun banning bills, is something of a joke. It is very awkward, slow to load and reload, and clumsy to fire as well as quite malfunction prone. The USAS-12, available with 10-shot box magazine or 20-shot drum, would be a good idea if it didn't weigh about 12 pounds and handle like an M-16 with a gland condition. In addition, we found this awkward weapon to not always be 100% reliable.

Some gunsmiths who specialize in combat shotguns are worthy of mention. Jon Tank at Tank's Rifle Shop does the nicest slickup of a Remington 870 this writer has yet seen. Jon is particularly good with M1A and Mini-14 rifles, as well.

Nu-Line Guns in Missouri does an excellent competition combat shotgun based on the Winchester Super X Model 1, the one gas-operated 12-gauge that may just be softer in recoil to start with than the Remington.

Mike LaRocca in my opinion is the best 1100/11-87 man around; he has done three of them for me and all have worked like thoroughbreds. By the time he is done with it, a 12-gauge kicks almost as mildly as a 20.

There are numerous other gunsmiths and armorers available, and any lack of mention implies no slight; rather, the above gunsmiths are the only ones of whose work the author has seen a great many specimens without a single bad one, and they are therefore the only ones he can competently recommend.

John Farnam demonstrates Hi-Standard 8113, first shotgun factory produced with extended magazines. No pump gun was slicker, but the design was breakage prone.

Ayoob has trouble taking Franchi SPAS-12 seriously. Gun had great shooting characteristics when it was "up and running," but was overly heavy and bulky, extremely complicated to operate, and experienced safety callback.

Author with Ithaca SKB, which Jeff Cooper called the best autoloading combat shotgun. Cooper may have ben right; gun is long out of production, however.

Combat Champion Raul Walters with customized Remington 100. Design fragility of 1100 with heavy loads was rectified in subsequent 11-87.

Richard "Skeeter" Skelton posed for author with his preferred home defense gun, an Ithaca model 37 12-gauge pump with extended magazine.

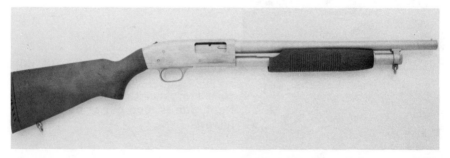

Mossberg 500 is a popular and ergonomic pump gun, author's choice in a 20 gauge and generally very functional in 12-gauge.

French policeman with Benelli Super 90 M3, convertible from semiautomatic to pump, a feature that does not impress the author.

Author considers Benelli M1 Super 90 to be the most ruggedly reliable, easily operated 12-gauge shotgun that can be purchased off the shelf. As shown, it is available with conventional or assault style stock.

Drum fed shotguns of the Street Sweeper type have not shown author good reliability, reload speed, or handling characteristics conducive to fast, accurate hits under stress.

Magazine-fed USAS-12 auto shotgun sounds great but test sample proved both awkward and unreliable.

Maverick, the low-price subsidiary of Mossberg, took over the latter's bullpup 12-gauge pump in the early '90s. A Maverick rep shows author the reduced-cost result at NRA Show, 1992. This unusual and very compact 12-gauge has proven itself reliable over time.

Chapter 9

Combat Shotgun Accessories

There are numerous factory-optional or aftermarket accessories for the combat shotgun. We'll examine them here in no particular order.

EXTENDED MAGAZINES. The extended tube adds little weight to the gun, and no significant extra bulk. More shots are generally better than fewer shots. This follows the theory of the gun itself, to wit: "It is better to have it and not need it than to need it and not have it."

This writer strongly recommends the extended magazine for several reasons. First, *the extended magazine functions as a unipod* and, as seen in the photos in the chapter on low position shooting, allows the gun to rest on the barricade while elevating the barrel sufficiently that the top of the barricade won't deflect or stop your fire, or worse, send particles and bouncing pellets back toward you. This greatly relieves fatigue during a long-term barricade situation, such as being a cop on a containment perimeter, or a citizen who has heard the alarm go off and is waiting for the intruders to enter the "safe room." This position also prevents trigger-jerking from pulling the muzzle down from the target: this writer has seen some pretty hefty mammals jerk low off the target in anticipation of 12-gauge recoil, but would defy Arnold Schwartzenegger to pull a 12-gauge shotgun down through a low cover barricade.

Second, *the extended magazine balances ammo needs with storage concerns.* When you disassemble your pump or auto shotgun, you'll see that the magazine spring extends almost from shoulder height to the ground. When it is compressed into a couple of inches by a fully loaded magazine-full of shells, one does not require a Masters in Metallurgical Engineering from CalTech to figure out that spring fatigue can take place, leading to a jam.

This is why most experts seasoned in the combat shotgun recommend that if it is kept constantly loaded, the magazine be downloaded, by one shell in a short (four-shell) magazine and by ore or two shells in a long (seven-to-nine-shell) magazine.

So loaded, the short magazine gun at cruiser ready will have but three shells on board and ready to deploy. A 20" barrel shotgun with extended magazine will have six on board, even when downloaded by one: *double* the in-gun capacity of the long-storage equivalent weapon with shorter magazine.

Finally, *there is the occasional, exceptional encounter where more rounds are needed.* John Shaw, firearms instructor and rifle/shotgun/pistol champion, recorded a case in which one of his police students became involved in a running gun battle, and finished the fast-breaking firefight in which there was no time to reload, with a shotgun round that wouldn't have been available to him if he hadn't had an extended magazine. In the infamous April 11, 1986 Miami gunfight, FBI agent Edmundo Mireles ran his 5-shot Remington 870 dry of 00 Magnum buckshot and had to draw his Smith & Wesson model 686 revolver, staggering into the kill zone to end the firefight with .38 slugs in his opponents' heads. No one will ever know whether an extended magazine that held three more shells in his 870 might have allowed him to finish the death duel from behind safe cover.

SHOTGUN SPEEDLOADERS. The first "shotgun speedloaders" didn't work worth a damn. The one now produced by ARMTEC is not bad, though it requires an attachment locked onto the receiver of the gun itself. True, the long tubular shell carriers are a pain in the butt to carry, but they make a lot of sense for those who won't be carrying them. By that I mean the armed citizen who prefers an empty gun stored separate from ammo.

If I had little kids in the house whom I couldn't trust around loaded guns, I would have my Remington 1100, mounted with this device, as part of my primary defense gun, and two four-round speedloaders in a separate location I could access quickly. Shove in the first, rack the action, and one is ready to go. Since my gun has the Choate magazine extender, the second 4-shell loader would slide in nicely once there was a round in the chamber, time permitting.

The ARMTEC is the only shotgun speedloader I can recommend at this writing.

SHELL-TO-GUN ATTACHMENTS. Spare shells attached to the off-side frame of the Remington shotgun, as produced by Adventurer's Outpost are handy indeed. They make more sense than "butt cuffs," which hold the shells on the stock. Alas, only the Remington shotgun at this writing can be retrofitted with frame-mounted shell carriers.

Those on the buttstock, available from several manufacturers, can be driven painfully into your face when you fire weak-handed. One police training manual actually stated that such shells should go on the inside of the stock, *guaranteeing* that you'll mash your maxillo-facial area upon firing. If one wants this sort of thing, SWAT/Viper produces a good buttstock carrier that has a foam-call flap that will shield the face if you fire weak-handed, and a loose shell or two rides along the toe of the stock, out of the way of the face but very quick to access. You can just take the old, simple, elastic Perry Ammo Sling and twist it around so the shells are along the bottom edge of the stock, for that matter; they may actually be quicker to get at from there, and they won't hurt your face anymore.

L.L. Baston makes a shell carrier that goes on the fore-end of an autoloading shotgun. It gets in the way for me and doesn't work nearly as well as other designs, but some people like it.

Avoid the shoulder straps with loops that carry spare shells. The sling will move with the shell as you try to withdraw the round, perhaps fatally slowing your reloading time, and it will swing heavily under the gun and pull it off target when you have to fire in an action situation.

SHOTGUN SLINGS. For the hunter or soldier, a sling makes a great deal of sense. For the combat shotgunner, it is situational. The sling will be handy in training, when you're standing around listening to lectures but ready to go back to the range. It is in dynamic situations that it creates problems.

The sling can snag on a door handle as you're exiting the cruiser, and on furniture as you're moving through a house, whether in home defense or police status. In a struggle for the gun, it's one more purchase-point an opponent can use to gain leverage.

A SWAT man may need it for rappelling and whatnot; the patrol officer and home defender will often find that the sling has more debits than credits.

This writer feels the best approach is a light carrying sling with QD (quick detachable) swivels. It can be kept in the kit bag or the glove compartment of the cruiser, rolled up and ready, and put on when needed. Otherwise, it should probably be left off the weapon.

LIGHT SOURCES. This writer did not believe in flashlights mounted on long guns until January 1991 for several good reasons.

They are bulky; they can go on by accident; since the activating switch is in the area you normally firmly grasp when entering danger situations; and, with the short, easy trigger on a shotgun, startle response can easily take place if you become careless and use the light for routine searching. If the finger closes on an off-safe trigger, you have just blown away whatever it was that startled you, which may not necessarily be a bad guy.

In 1/91, however, the author was running with the Special Reaction Team of the Palm Beach County (FL) Sheriff's Department on a couple of drug raids. As we deployed from the unmarked van on one of them, a scout shouted that there was a man in a window of the target house. His silhouette was visible, but no one could see if he had a weapon in his hand or not.

The team leader had a SureFire light on the forestock of his Benelli Super 90 shotgun, an attachment that is standard equipment on PBSO SRT's MP5 submachineguns as well. He beamed the suspect, who spun back away from the blinding light. A moment later, a concussion grenade went off, the drug house was breached, and all inside were arrested uneventfully.

I went home and ordered a SureFire attachment for my personal MP5, and paid for it out of my own pocket. The submachinegun may have belonged to the department, but my backside belonged to me.

The flashlight is a useful attachment, but one *should not let it become the standard search illumination tool*. In that situation, a handgun in one fist and a flashlight in the other will work much better. If you are a home defender, remember this simple fact: *If the alarm has gone off and you think someone might have gotten into your kids' room, a flashlight attached to your weapon means you have to point your loaded shotgun at your own children to ascertain that they are all right.*

LASER SIGHTS. A *flashlight* attached to your weapon allows you to blind an opponent, and to guarantee his identification as a hostile target before you fire. *A laser-dot sight* allows neither. It will only intimidate someone who happens to be looking down checking his chest for little red spots — unlikely in real life. It can go out if the batteries fail, or if a sharp blow to the weapon or sighting unit knocks things out of contact.

The laser would make sense for the security guard in a truly armored truck who had to assess his target through one Lexan sighting window and fire through another, separate shooting port. Consider the laser's use on a SWAT operation.

Two of you with laser-sighted weapons enter a room. An armed Bad Guy is holding a child hostage in front of him. You and your partner both swing your weapons up. One dot appears on the suspect, *and one on the kid.* Which is yours? Which is your partner's? Who should fire before the bad guy kills you both? How about you just aim your damn shotgun at the suspect's head, decapitate him, and solve the problem swiftly and surely with sighting technology that has existed since the dawn of remote-control small arms, and has proven quite effective?

If you get the impression that the author thinks lasers are losers, you are 100% correct. If you've already bought one, however, all is not lost; go to the SPCA and rescue a kitten. You and the kitty will have hours of fun as the little furball chases the red dot all over the floor and up the walls. A laser sight is, however, an overly expensive feline exercise toy.

ON-PERSON AMMO CARRIERS. Probably the most practical on-the-body shotshell carrier for combat is the plastic unit designed for John Satterwhite by Bill Rogers and produced today by Safariland. It allows two-by-two loading of 12-ga. shells only, and clips quickly on and off a dress belt, a duty gunbelt, or the straps on a bullet-resistant vest. They are too inexpensive not to have, and your local gunshop that carries Safariland products can get them for you.

The best *fixed* shotshell carrier — i.e., one that loops instead of snaps onto the belt — is available from Elmer MacEvoy at the Leather Arsenal. Made for 20-ga. *or* 12-ga., and custom-available for any other size, the Leather Arsenal 2X2 carries four shells in a more firmly fixed position than the Rogers design. In short, if I know there may be trouble I strap on a MacEvoy 2X2; I keep the Rogers carriers around for when I don't know whether there'll be trouble or not, but I might have to suit up quick.

John Shaw was the first expert to notice that a .45-size auto pistol magazine pouch could hold two shotgun shells where one magazine would go before. This can sometimes be a useful expedient, certainly better than fumbling in one's pockets for spare shells.

RECOIL REDUCING DEVICES. They are all of use and if it's a personally owned shotgun, put on as many as you can afford: the less it kicks, the faster you can shoot it straight against multiple targets. The author favors Magna-Port's "Pro-Porting," stocks with mercury inserts, and particularly the Harrt's retrofit stock.

SIGHTS. Perhaps the most over-rated and overly discussed shotgun accessory, optional sights become an issue only when predictable range extends. As stated elsewhere, the large-ring peep sight that Jeff Cooper dubbed "ghost ring" is probably the best for an all-purpose combat weapon that may be used at intermediate to long ranges; the simple bead remains the fastest and therefore the best for employment of buckshot at across-the-room, home-defense distances.

The true Shotgun Speedloader has long been sought.

Overextended screw from other side of receiver-attached scope mount tore this shooter's palm open. Gun, which bears no fault, is Mossberg 500. Not all add-ons are "user-friendly."

Oversize bolt handle makes sense on Remington 1100 or 11-87; cutaway shell carrier for key insertion to clear stoppage does not and can be potentially dangerous.

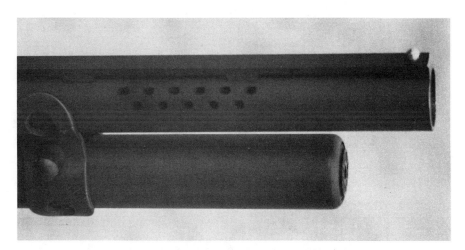

MagnaPort Pro-Porting makes sense on any shotgun. So does white bead front sight on vent rib, and extended Choate magazine with support brace, seen here on LaRocca Custom Remington 1100 12-ga. Photo courtesy *Guns* magazine and Frank Muggianu.

Home-made extended magazine seems to work on this Browning Automatic-5, but more to the point, so does the "bird cage" style recoil compensator seen at muzzle. This shooter is rapid-firing 12-gauge rifled slugs at Second Chance "BCBC" match.

Slings are handy for range, parades, inspections, and sport use in the field, but can snag on objects when exiting cruiser or in home defense situation.

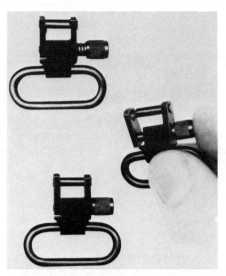

If one must have sling on shotgun, it should have QD (quick-detachable) sling swivels like these.

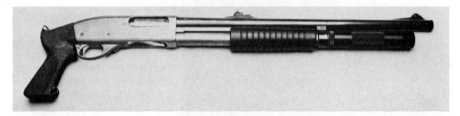

Let's analyze the four options seen on this Remington 870. The Choate retrofit fore-end will generally give more efficient and positive handling operation. The light that replaces an extended magazine has pros and cons. Pistol grip stock is a poor choice, and makes nearly useless the rifled sights that might have made sense with a fixed-stock shotgun for long range slug use.

Choate extender brings 26" barrel Remington 1100 to 10-shot capacity. If maneuverability is not a problem, this weapon will prove most formidable.

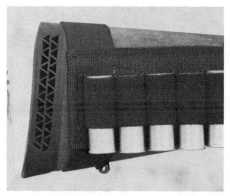

"Butt cuffs" for spare ammo are admittedly handy, but can be a problem when shooter has to go "ambidex." Padded "SWAT/Viper" style cuff, units that carry shells along toe of stock, or SpeedFeed stock may be more desirable. Recoil pad, on the other hand, can be most welcome.

Many shotgunners swear by Edwards Recoil Reducer. Here, in cutaway, is a double installation.

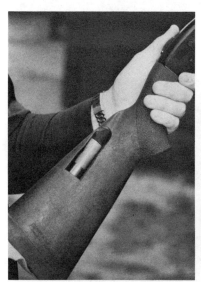

SpeedFeed stock on Mossberg 500 is not the fastest of reloading systems, but is handy and practical and does not interfere with firing in any way. Thumb safety on top tang is the most ergonomic safety catch design.

Modern shotgun speedloaders, fitted with adapter mounted on gun, *do* work. Adapter interferes with some scope mounts, however. Nylon carrier puts two 4-shell speedloaders at one's hip.

Three accessories the author cannot recommend highly enough are shown with this S&W 12-ga. pump. Ghost ring sight by Mossberg, popularized by Jeff Cooper, is available as separate part for retrofit to any shotgun. Choate oversize safety catch reduces fumbling under stress. Leather Arsenal 2X2 shotshell carrier is best design the author has yet seen.

Mundane in appearance stock, the lightweight and virtually unbreakable "conventional style" Choate shotgun may well be the best such retrofit. Chief R. Lary demonstrates it here on a Remington 12-ga. 870.

Shown on the barrel of one of the author's Mossberg 500s, the FireFly sight by Julio Santiago is low profile, extremely fast for bucksot, and quite accurate for rifled slugs. It is also cost effective.

Recommended by seasoned hunters in the 19th Century, and rediscovered and popularized today by Jeff Cooper, the large aperture or "ghost ring" rear sight allows maximum speed with buckshot in close, maximum accuracy with slugs at any distance. One looks through the ring and ignores it, focusing on the front sight that will automatically be centered therein by the normal human eye.

Tasco Pro-Point allows regular sight
picture beneath the scope, or stress point
index of front and rear rifle sight through
the lense.

Chapter 10

Safe Administrative Handling of the Shotgun

Administrative handling of a gun means loading and unloading it, checking to see if it' loaded or unloaded, and carrying it around in situations other than those in which immediate firing is a likelihood.

On the training range, LFI requires that the shotguns will be unloaded, actions open, muzzle up, and on-safe whenever the student is not actually about to shoot. If the gun must be laid down, it is not rested against anything vertically (except a gun rack designed for the purpose, that will prevent an accidental fall of the weapon). The gun will be laid on the ground, closed side of the action down to reduce dirt's chances of getting into the mechanism. Slings are fine, so long as the muzzles remain up.

The time will come when the shooter has no sling, and has to hold a loaded gun while doing something with both hands, such as putting on a forgotten pair of ear or eye protectors. Some have suggested "hugging" the shotgun to the chest, with the muzzle up; however, the author fears this will increase the likelihood of a slip. The shotgun will fall straight down, landing on its butt; the firing pin may bounce in its channel; and the resultant accidental discharge could decapitate the shooter.

We teach instead our whimsically-titled "John Holmes Method." The comb on the stock rests in the cleft of the buttocks as the flat side of the stock is grasped between the thighs, the muzzle pointing down. While this could plug the muzzle of a long barrel gun in snow, it generally works fine for small to average or taller people on a dry range, using shotguns with 24" or shorter barrels.

One must adapt to local custom. Teaching in Great Britain, where "practical shotgun" is a much more developed combat sport than in the U.S. relatively speaking, the universal rule is that the gun muzzles will be down rather than up. The author ground his teeth continually during each such program.

Accustom yourself to checking the gun by sight and feel. Probe the firing chamber with a pinky to make sure it is empty; palpate the magazine tube as well as looking at it to make sure you are touching only the follower of an empty magazine, and not the head of a live shotgun shell.

The finger should be kept out of the trigger guard at all times except when planning to fire. This simple precaution would probably reduce firearms accidents by more than half, in and of itself.

Similarly, follow always the cardinal twin rules of safe firearms handling: ALWAYS TREAT THE GUN AS IF IT WAS FULLY LOADED, AND NEVER ALLOW THE MUZZLE TO POINT AT ANYTHING YOU ARE NOT PREPARED TO SEE DESTROYED.

Be scrupulously careful about what type of ammunition you are using. Many people have been severely injured when their shotguns blew up with handloaded ammunition.

A twenty gauge shotgun shell (industry color code: Yellow) is of a size that, if dropped into the chamber of a 12-gauge shotgun, the entire shell can slip down the barrel, stopping partway toward the muzzle. When a regular twelve gauge shell (industry color code: Red) slips easily into the chamber and is then fired, an explosion will occur at the location of the 20-gauge shell that can amputate your forward hand, and blind you and others nearby with shrapnel.

ALWAYS wear OSHA-rated eye protection when you are shooting, or are around people who shoot. When firing at steel targets or bowling pins, be aware that there might be a bounceback. If your protective lenses do not have side shields, never turn sideways when on such a range, but instead always face the targets with the glasses in place, or have your back to the targets. A fragment that will cause a mere laceration of the forehead or the back of the neck can and will destroy a human eyeball.

ALWAYS wear the best possible hearing protection when firing any gun. A 12-gauge shotgun has a particularly deafening blast when short combat barrels are combined with powerful combat loads. Many, many people have lost their hearing partially or wholly due to sport shooting or firearms training without proper hearing protection. The author exclusively uses Wolf Ears, active hearing protectors that reduce the loudest sound to about what you would hear through regular muffs when firing a standard .38 Special revolver round. However, small sounds are amplified. This allows the range officer to be able to pick up the slightest sign of a shooter having a problem. For hunting, it has allowed the author to pinpoint the location of animals in the bush before seasoned trackers and bushmen could spot them. For a tactical situation, they are ideal; they allow the Good Guy to even hear a man breathing farther away than could be heard by the naked ear, and to pinpoint exactly the direction of the sound, yet the most deafening blast will be reduced to a harmless level that causes no injury, and does not even temporarily stun out a vital sensory acquisition that could make the difference between living and dying in the next few minutes. Wolf Ears and information thereon are available from Armor of New Hampshire, PO Box 122, Concord, NH 03301.

Finally, remember that we know more about lead poisoning related to firearms handling than we used to. Always wash the hands and mouth area thoroughly before eating after you've been shooting, using cool or lukewarm soapy water. (Hot water can open the pores and allow substances to "leach in.") When you return home from shooting, immediately put the clothes you were wearing in the wash pile and shower and shampoo before donning fresh clothes. When cleaning guns, observe the same precautions; the author suggests a gauze face mask (scrubbing the bore will put tiny, inhaleable lead particles in the air) and wearing rubber or plastic gloves. Carbon tetrachloride type sprays are best used outdoors during the gun cleaning process.

Shuto (karate chop) technique opens Benelli 121 action to drop in first round; later modification and still later Super 90 had different "manual of arms."

Pincer hook technique scoops two shells from Satterwhite carrier . . .

. . . and swing toward loading gate of Benelli 121.

Assorted vertical carries, ASLET '91. Shooter at left uses LH hip carry, supported by free hand; George Voltz, center, uses low profile carry; Tony Gregory, right, uses thigh carry. L to R, 12-gauge autos are Beretta, Pistol-grip Super 90, and standard Super 90.

To keep hands free, Brian Felter likes this "hug the baby" hold. It makes sense in deep snow.

Committed to police training, Beretta sent tens of 1200 FP auto shotguns, and more importantly chief instructor Brian Felter, to ASLET. Learning nomenclature and weapon's manual of arms is critical from the beginning.

FBI chamber load with Benelli 121: Dominant right thumb holds back bolt handle while left palm is about to slap first shell in.

ASLET attendees learn Brian Felter's hooked fingers technique to examine chamber of autoloading shotgun to confirm/deny presence of a shell.

Safe administrative unloading of auto shotgun is demonstrated w/Remington 1100 LT-20. Butt braced on right thigh, right thumb draws back bolt, ejecting chambered round into waiting left palm . . .

. . . gun is now tilted onto its side, and next round up is rolled off shell lift, out the ejection port, and into waiting hand. Magazine is then unloaded through loading port at bottom of receiver.

If shotgun has no sling and shooter needs both hands for earmuffs or whatever, LFI teaches this whimsically titled "John Holmes" technique. On-safe shotguns is clasped between thighs, comb of stock resting in cleft of buttocks, keeping muzzle in safe direction while hands are free.

86

Peter Dayton demonstrates hand change for ambidextrous shooting. He begins with Larocca Custom twenty gauge 1100 at shoulder . . .

Gun hand comes forward to rear of fore-end.

Left foot moves to rear as left hand falls back to trigger group.

Weapon is now mounted at left shoulder.

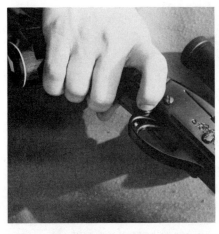

With conventional crossbolt safety set up for right handed use, tip of index finger of firing hand is used thus to put gun in "fire" mode.

Reaching under the trigger guard with middle finger is easiest way to achieve the left to right button push that on-safes the gun.

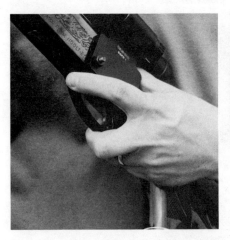

When gun with right hand safety is used left handed this movement of middle finger is fastest and most positive way to take the gun off safe.

Working standard safety left handed, left index finger is most naturally situated to on-safe the gun.

Chapter 11

Shotgun Grasp: The Proper Hold

Most people put the shotgun butt in the wrong position when they "mount" the weapon, that is, bring it up to aim. The grasp of a gun is the foundation of technique, and if it is done badly, everything will go downhill from there.

Some people bring the gun's buttplate to the juncture between the deltoid (shoulder) muscle and the bicep. Recoil will now crush the sensitive brachial nerve between the butt of the gun and the underlying humerus bone. The more muscular shooter is not immune, indeed, sharp muscle definition becomes a "braille guide" that actually slides the gun butt to this sensitive area.

A majority of shooters who have not learned the proper technique will instinctively try to place the butt against the rounded mass of the shoulder muscle. Unfortunately, recoil will drive the gun butt down the rounded edge of the deltoid and into the brachial plexus, as described above.

The butt belongs in what shotgun masters call "the shoulder pocket," which actually is not on the shoulder, but *between the pectoral muscle and the deltoid*. However, for this to work properly, *the elbow on that side must be raised, to shoulder level or slightly higher*.

Try this simple exercise. Place the edge of the heel of your non-dominant hand on the rounded part of your shoulder muscle. Push hard; you will feel it slip down into the brachial nerve area between deltoid and bicep. The same will happen with the shotgun's butt upon recoil.

Now, place the same hand the same way between the pectoral muscle and the deltoid. You should be able to feel your collarbone. No, we're not going to fracture your easily-broken clavicle with the recoil. Keep your hand where it is, and raise the elbow on the firing side. Feel how the heavy muscle comes up over the collarbone? Now replicate recoil again; notice that the hand is trapped in a valley of muscle, as the gun butt will be, and can no longer slide down the arm.

The muscle in question is not particularly sensitive. This is why both men and primates can beat on their chests. It is also why this is the location of choice at which to place the butt of a gun that kicks as hard as an elephant rifle.

The gun must be *pulled in tight to the shoulder.* When it is held tight, the recoil impulse may be unpleasant but it will not significantly injure; it is as if the kick passed through the body and into the open air behind. If, however, the amateur succumbs even for one shot to the instinctive desire to "get this thing away from me," not only magnified pain but actual injury can result. This is because, once the gun butt is so much as 1/64th of an inch away from the body, it will now strike *with impact,* and the impact will feel like being buttstroked by an enemy soldier.

With the conventional shotgun stock, as opposed to the vertical pistol grip of the so-called "assault stock," thumb placement can be a concern. Most of the people who have sustained black eyes, glasses knocked off, or broken or bloody noses when firing a 12-gauge shotgun, were not hurt by the shotgun itself. They were hurt by their own thumb.

It is human nature to curl the thumb around any heavy object we pick up. We will naturally grab a shotgun like this. However, it is recoiling into the shoulder, which is a moveable joint, and the head is not moving reciprocally with it; therefore, the thumb is what comes back and "bops you on the beezer."

The best place for the thumb, then, is pointed at the muzzle and resting atop the receiver. This is the position it would be in to operate a top-tang safety, as on the Mossberg 500 or 590 pump gun, or a conventional double barrel shotgun.

Once the *grasp,* the hold, of the weapon has been correctly accomplished, the next concern is *stance,* the total body position. We'll begin, in the next chapter, with the standing position and tactically relevant variations.

Chapter 12

Recoil Management

It is the brutal recoil of the 12-gauge combat shotgun that makes it such a difficult weapon with which to gain confidence and competence. Light trap and skeet loads can be fired all day without ill effect. However, the powerful high-base buckshot and rifled slug loads normally used for combat are another proposition altogether.

For one civil trial (in which, through poor police department policy and training, a female officer had been crippled for life by a shoulder injury sustained in departmental shooting qualification) it was determined that by a commonly used industry formula, her department's shotgun and 12-ga. buckshot load delivered 78 foot pounds of recoil energy. That exactly equalled the recoil of the .375 Holland and Holland Magnum cartridge, generally considered an "elephant rifle." Thus, the person firing a light combat shotgun in rapid fire with high powered anti-personnel loads can be said to literally be rapid-firing an elephant gun.

Anything that imparts pain to the student in training will make him or her hesitant to use it on the street. This sort of punishment can also cause the learned, subconscious habit of convulsively jerking not only the trigger finger, but the whole body, forward against the anticipated recoil, causing the shot to miss the intended target.

This writer has seen two "training victims" with permanent injuries to the shoulder from combat shotgun shooting, and numerous others with bloody noses, one broken finger, one with two broken teeth, and countless with massive bruises of the face, chest, and arms. All of these injuries could have been prevented with proper techniques and training.

Different Approaches

Big people, not surprisingly, can recover from recoil more rapidly than little people. Combat tactician and instructor John Farnam once observed that persons who weigh over 180 pounds seem to take to the shotgun more readily than those who weigh less. Few people, however, will take up weight training just so they can become more proficient with the defensive shotgun.

Smaller bore shotguns are one answer. While it is a rare police department that will adopt a lighter weapon than a 12-gauge (though there have been exceptions), civilians are often wise to go to a lighter gun. The 16-gauge shotgun has seldom been experimented with, but the 20-gauge offers light, easy handling combined with minimal (for a shotgun) recoil, and perhaps twice the destructive power of a .44 Magnum handgun. For close combat work, adoption of the 20-gauge may be the fastest route to finding a combat shotgun that is easily managed.

Recoil control devices offer much potential. Assorted muzzle brakes of the "bird cage" style do reduce kick, although they also extend the length of the weapon. ProPorting by MagnaPort is easily and quickly installed, and is the most practical for a police department weapon; while it does not reduce impact to the shoulder, it does keep the muzzle down and enhance accurate rapid fire. The privately-owned weapon can be fitted with springloaded or mercury recoil reducers in the stock.

Recoil pads cushion kick, some better than others; the best seem to be the current generation made of Sorbothane.

Lighter loads within the same gauge can be employed. Until recently, this required handloaded shotgun shells, or low-base birdshot loads that would have had limited anti-personnel effectiveness. In the late '80s, however, Remington pioneered a reduced velocity 12-ga. 00 buckshot load whose pellets travelled several hundred feet per second slower than those of a full load. The police market yawned. Federal Cartridge Corporation, however, brought out a functionally identical shell they dubbed "*tactical buckshot*", and it became a runaway bestseller in the law enforcement market. It was a great moment in advertising.

At this writing, there are not yet enough documented shootings with the reduced velocity 00 load to get a handle on its stopping power, but it is reasonable to assume that it will penetrate enough but not too much – indeed, will not have the tendency of full-power 00 buckshot to overpenetrate at close range – and will cause ample damage to fulfill its stopping power mission. This load will work in most semiautomatic shotguns, but not necessarily all; it should be tested amply in the individual weapon before life is trusted to it. Naturally, it presents no feeding problems in slide-action shotguns.

Cumulative Effects

Naturally, the more effort is made toward recoil reduction, the easier the gun/ammo combination is to manage. The writer's standard Ithaca pump with plastic buttplate is something he can manage with heavy loads due to experience and training, but still an unpleasant experience. His LaRocca Custom Remington 1100 with mercury recoil reducer, Sorbothane pad, and ProPorting is pleasant to shoot with the same heavy loads, and with tactical buckshot, is downright fun. By the same token, a novice would find the above-fitted Ithaca nearly unmanageable, the custom Remington controllable if not necessarily pleasurable. All things are relative. It follows that, since the combat shotgun is a tool that will only be employed "for real" when innocent human life is at stake, every effort spent to make the weapon more controllable and more user-friendly is an effort that stands to be rewarded in the most priceless commodity.

The Technique Factor

Technique is probably more important than any mechanical factor. A round of buckshot or a rifled slug fired from the hardest-kicking shotgun will be better managed by a user with good technique than will the highest-tech reduced-kick gun held wrong by an amateur or someone who has been given obsolete training.

The techniques presented in this book – the StressFire system for the combat shotgun – have been proven to allow small people, weak people, and even people with injured shoulders to effectively utilize the hardest-kicking weapons of this type. If recoil is your primary concern, the techniques to concentrate on are "Pec-Vest" and "High Tuck."

Chapter 13

Women and Combat Shotguns

Women are more sensitive to heavy shotgun recoil then men. They have less upper body mass and strength, less muscular padding over the area where the recoil is felt. Their arms are generally shorter and the guns are often too long for them. This requires them to cantilever their shoulders back for strength, which takes them off balance against the recoil. See photos.

There are, of course, fixes. Petite women in particular will appreciate the 20-gauge shotgun, which with buck and slug loads is quite ample for home defense.

The shotgun stock can be cut to fit by any good gunsmith who has a reputation for doing this sort of work. Remington and other manufacturers make Youth Models of guns like the LT-20. These have shorter stocks, and better fit small statured persons. Male or female, small statured persons will also benefit proportionally more from recoil reducing devices than bigger people, and this is especially true of modifications like MagnaPort which,unlike the mercury units in the stock, do not add to the weight of the gun.

Any man who laughs at women who have trouble with man-size shotguns should spend an afternoon trying to do rapid maneuvers with a 12-pound USAS-12, or a 10 1/2 pound SPAS-12 or Roadblocker Mag-10. He will quickly "raise his consciousness" as to the problems a petite female has with an 8 1/2 pound 12-gauge shotgun with long stock.

One police department in the midwest purchased shortened-stock 20-gauge shotguns for their female officers, painting the stocks yellow to color-coordinate with the 20-gauge shells to prevent ammunition mixups. The male officers who suffered from testosterone poisoning immediately coined a nickname for the new weapons: "cunt guns." Nonetheless, the concept worked well in the field.

X number of police (or, for that matter, civilian) instructors feel a need to denigrate those who are not exactly like them. The bias is sometimes sexist, sometimes racist, and always stupid. The whole concept of the fighting firearm is one of an "equalizer." If I am down and in trouble, I want the brother or sister officer who is racing in to back me up to be armed with the weapon he or she is most competent and most confident with.

The instructor's function is not to create clones of himself; it is to assist his students in finding the path that will make them most skillfully and efficiently capable of performing the predictable mission at hand. The writer knows a large number of hefty male shotgun experts – including one particularly rowdy 300+ pound male – who would be delighted to take the individual who coined the term "cunt gun" into the alley behind the local cop bar and "raise his consciousness." If that approach is too self-defeatingly macho, that individual is invited to shoot a speed match in public against women like Barbara Budnar, using full-load 12-gauge…if he has the capital to cover the side bets.

Female more than male students appreciate the High Tuck method, especially when combined with an assault stock shotgun whose pistol grip allows the more delicate female wrist to be firmly locked for maximum strength and control. Women also do extremely well with the Pec-Vest technique. We are reminded that care must be taken to place the gun *above* the breast.

The aggressive wide-straddled StressFire stance allows a female to maximize two natural advantages vis-a-vis males: her relatively stronger lower limbs, and her lower center of gravity. With her forward leg sharply flexed and its muscles taut, her lower body can support much of the shotgun's weight and make up for her relative lack of upper body strength.

A visit to a match like Second Chance will show that many fit, athletic women can handle a 12-gauge shotgun better than the average large male police officer. Top female contestants like Debbie Higgins, Bonnie Young, and Barb Budnar have given countless male competitors a much-needed attitude adjustment and testosterone reduction.

A final technique is available to the recoil sensitive, male or female, that will only work in a well-planned home-defense scenario. The gun is lined up with the anticipated point of entry and its butt braced firmly against a hard wall or door frame. The armpit goes over the stock in a high tuck type of technique. The stock takes a lot of stress upon recoil and may eventually crack or break, but no recoil is transmitted to the shooter.

One Texas firearms instructor, Charlie Reese, taught this to a battered woman who was being terrorized by her ex-husband. When the abuser broke through the window of her home, screaming that he would kill her and ignoring her warnings, the woman used this technique to fire a fast double-tap. Both blasts of 00 buck caught the suspect full in the chest, killing him instantly. The grand jury exonerated the woman, and at least one investigating police officer enthusiastically complimented her ingenuity, coolness and marksmanship.

The gun is too heavy, the stock too long, and this courageous but petite lady is going . . .

. . . going . . .

Janet Hartman, instructor at Ohio Peace Officer Training Academy, demonstrates use of the High Tuck by petite female. Shotgun is full-power Remington 870 12-ga.

. . . nearly gone with three shots of 00 Buck from recoil-softened Remington 1100. Note that by last photo there is a shadow under her forward shoe: her forward foot has literally been lifted off the ground by three fast applications of 78 ft-lb. of recoil.

The Shadow Knows: camera sees from front angle, and shadow shows from side, that petite Martha Randall has to cantilever her shoulders back to aim 12-gauge pump with full length stock. She projects defeatist body language, and will probably be out of control if not on her back after the first shot.

Switching to Remington LT-20 auto, Martha can easily hold up the front end of a 5 1/2 lb. 20-gauge. Her upper body weight now commits aggressively forward, giving her excellent recoil control *and* "body language deterrent factor."

Author finds that compact guns and large dogs are an excellent combination for petite women, as Martha demonstrates with Remington 1100 LT-20 and Jeremiah Puppybeast.

Muscle tone, technique, and gun fit must combine for a compact women to control a 12-gauge shotgun in rapid fire with powerful combat loads. Here Bonnie Young shows winning form, with a Remington 1100 built to her specifications, at Second Chance.

Ace firearms instructor Cathy Lane supervises as a female officer learns to handle the Beretta 12-gauge auto shotgun. Note the aggressive forward body posture of student.

Chapter 14

Closest Combat

For close-range maneuvers, the handgun offers more flexibility than any long gun, and the short submachinegun offers more maneuverability than any other long gun; as the scale descends, the 14" barrel shotgun (its barrel cut level with a four-shell magazine tube) will be more maneuverable than any *other* repeating shotgun.

Firing from the hip, once taught as a standard police procedure for ranges of seven yards and in, has long since been discredited. The history of the technique in action showed it to be more likely to miss than to hit. This is because, with violent movement occurring on both sides of a real-life gunfight, the "body position index" that can work well on a static target is no longer able to line up the weapon with the ducking and weaving opponent. Virtually all instructors competent and confident enough to actually demonstrate a technique live-fire to their students and expect the students to perform to a minimum live-fire standard, have abandoned the hip-shooting techniques.

This writer was present with Robert Schwartz of the American Society of Law Enforcement Trainers when a municipal police department attempted to qualify with this technique at seven to ten yards. We both saw officers who not only missed the targets, but missed the entire backstop. When the guns were brought to the shoulders, however, the same officers hit their targets, and did so rapidly, even from considerably greater distances.

The shotgun is normally carried in a high ready or port arms position. From here, it is no slower to bring the butt up to the shoulder, using the weapon as it was designed to be used, than to bring the muzzle down to the hip level, which is an unnatural position from which to fire a long gun.

The High Tuck mentioned elsewhere in this book is the fastest possible technique for close quarters. Since the gun is snapped from high ready or port arms into the armpit, both the stock and the muzzle have a shorter axis to travel before the shot is fired.

Low ready position, sometimes called "Rhodesian ready," starts with the muzzle slightly down and the butt already at the shoulder. It is as fast as, or faster than, even the high tuck since the weapon is already mounted and only a very slight muzzle lift has to be accomplished to achieve a guaranteed index on the target. Low ready, while safe for the range (indeed, safer than high ready since an accidental discharge sends the shot into the dirt instead of over the backstop of the range), it is not ideal for close-quarters employment for two reasons.

First, the gun muzzle is now level with furniture in whatever building the Good Guy might be searching. As it bumps, Start Reflex can cause the flexor muscles, which are stronger than extensor muscles, to close; when the muscles in question are those of the trigger finger, a shot can be fired. At best, the officer stuns his own hearing and gives his position away; at worst, he blows his own foot off.

Second, if the officer is attacked from a hiding place or from the darkness in close quarters, he has very little leverage at low ready with which to raise his weapon to fire, or to retain control of the shotgun. As a National Instructor (certifying trainer of other instructors) in the Lindell Method of Weapon Retention through the National Law Enforcement Training Center, this writer can categorically state that low ready is a much more difficult position to defend against a disarming attempt than high ready. This is true with any firearm and is especially true of the long gun, as was first pointed out in 1983 in "StressFire."

The high ready gives you much more strength and flexibility for retaining the weapon, with little or no loss in ability to employ the gun effectively if shooting becomes necessary.

Note that in weapon retention, the pistol grip assault stock becomes a serious liability. Any opponent who has hold of the outer ends of the gun and levers back, jams the legitimate owner's thumb joint in the juncture between grip and trigger guard. Your only choice is whether you let go before or after your thumb is torn out of the socket. With the conventional shotgun stock, your hand is in a much stronger position to resist that movement.

With a pistol grip only, the situation is even worse. A long barrel pistol is easier to take away from someone than a short barrel pistol; a pistol grip only shotgun is, for weapon retention purposes, an *extremely* long-barreled pistol. At least with the assault stock, a Good Guy with excellent reflexes can let go of the pistol grip and attempt to grip the main stock for retention; this option is not possible with the pistol grip only design.

Even at the closest distances, the higher the gun is to line of sight, the more likely it will be that your shot will strike a vital part of the body that will instantly neutralize your lethal attacker. If the suspect is too close for you to do that, he is probably *so* close that you can *thrust-fire*, that is, *thrust the muzzle of the gun into his body while you simultaneously pull the trigger.*

Another chapter of this book graphically illustrates the degree to which ballistic damage is magnified when the shot is delivered at muzzle contact distance. The wound becomes literally explosive in its characteristics. While a semiautomatic pistol can be jammed by flesh blown back into the mechanism, and even a revolver's cylinder can fail to rotate for a second shot if enough flesh is blown back into the cylinder/chamber area, the author knows of no case on record in which a shotgun has been jammed by muzzle contact with any part of a human body when the round was discharged. Yes, there will be more pressure in the barrel, but instead of the barrel blowing up, that part of the body will; ordnance steel is stronger than flesh and bone.

It should go without saying that at very close combat distance, the probability of a disarming attempt by a homicidal offender is great. A long gun like a rifle or shotgun is easier to take away from a defender than a handgun, for two reasons: long gun disarming is more widely known to the public thanks to military training, and the longer gun gives the disarmer much more leverage. It follows, then, that weapon retention training is critically important to anyone who takes a gun of any kind, and particularly a two-handed weapon, into a danger situation.

Front snap technique. Under the watchful eye of rangemaster, Ayoob "kills" 15-yard Pepper Popper with Benelli 121 00 Buck load while racing through vertical cover point of assault course at Missouri State Championships. Note halo of fragmenting lead around steel target, spent casing in mid-air in line with Popper's bottom joint. Front snap hits at this distance and speed cannot be guaranteed. Photo courtesy Chapman Academy.

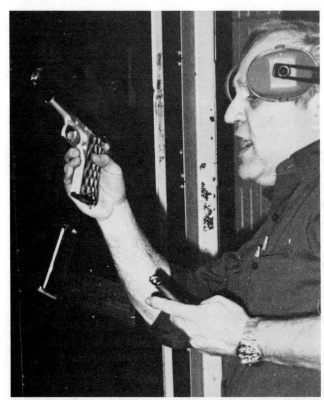

Bill Groce of OPOTA, lethal shootout vet and SWAT man, is shown here demonstrating combat reload of Colt .45 pistol. Author considers him the leading developer of modern close-combat firing techniques with shotguns.

This French national policeman demonstrates "underarm assault" position with Benelli Super 90 M-3, convertible to pump or auto fire.

Halfway between hip-shooting and underarm assault, this officer's technique will only work on a static shooting range. Photo courtesy Day/Night Sights.

"Keep the eye on the front sight," warns the Beretta Pro, Brian Felter. Starting in a high ready position . . .

. . . the sight will be directly in line with your eye and the opponent, even if you begin with your eyes off the danger . . .

. . . and a quick snap to the shoulder delivers instant hit without having to consciously line up the sights, which are already unconsciously in line. Felter is aiming at a target beyond the FBI "Q" that is visible in photo; gun is Beretta 1200 FP.

Close combat includes weapon retention. Instructor Rick Devoid grabs Ayoob's assault stock pump with pistol grip, and "pinwheel disarm" crushes juncture of stock and pistol grip against base of thumb, forcing him to let go or have thumb socket torn out.

When attacker tries same technique with conventionally stocked shotgun, here a Remington 1100, author can simply "go with the flow," ripping loose from attacking hand and crushing attacker's groin with forward buttstroke . . .

. . . or pivot outward and deliver attack-stopping buttstroke to temple. Since attempted disarm must presume destructive intent, this level of force is warranted in retaining weapon against a criminal attempting a disarm.

Chapter 15

Low Positions

Situationally, the defender often has more horizontal cover than vertical cover. While a high, flat wall would be horizontal cover, it would allow a standing position. However, most horizontal cover tends to be *low* cover: auto hoods, stone walls, windowsills, etc. This mandates that the shooter be able to fire from a *low* position.

Tactically, Lethal Force Institute defines two types of cover. When there is time to perceive the danger and get to a position that allows you to monitor the danger area, maximize personal shielding, and even perhaps support your weapon or your stance, you will be taking *ensconced* cover. When you are attacked without warning and seek to immediately get something large and solid between you and the threat, you are taking *reactive* cover.

The most useful *ensconced low cover position* is KNEELING. Unfortunately, most people will attempt to adapt the conventional rifle marksman's kneeling position to the shotgun. This can have disastrous results, since the powerful combat shotgun can have up to twice the recoil of the .308 or .30/06 class of battle rifle.

If you have tucked your rear heel under your buttocks and the upper body is relatively erect, don't be surprised if the first round, or certainly the second, of high-based buckshot or rifled slug ammo knocks you backward onto the ground. If you have braced your elbow forward of your knee, don't be surprised if you short-stroke your pump gun after the first shot, either; this position restricts arm movement.

To effectively fire the combat-loaded shotgun from kneeling, *the shoulders must still be aggressively forward of the pelvis* if recoil control, indeed the position itself, is to be maintained. If firing a pump shotgun, *the elbow of the forward arm must be above the knee, clear to operate freely.* Finally, *the lower body must be in an extremely strong position* such as "artillery kneeling" or "double kneeling."

Lethal Force Institute developed the term "artillery kneeling" for a position in which the non-shooting side leg is sharply bent, the calf jack-knifed all the way in until it touches the back of the thigh, with the ball of the foot on the ground and the heel under the pelvis. The rear leg is stretched out behind the shooter, with the inside of the foot down on the ground, like the trailer of a howitzer. This gives very strong support against the combat shotgun's heavy recoil.

LFI named an alternative technique "double kneeling." The shooter drops to *both* knees, the gun-side of the body quartered back away from the target about 45° with a conventional mount of the gun, or squared to the target when using the Pec-Vest technique.

In either of the above techniques, it remains important to keep the shoulders forward of the hips. While these techniques are so strong it is almost physically impossible for the shooter to be knocked backward (in double kneeling, the bent lower legs function like V-springs) the muzzle can still rise, drastically slowing response of second and subsequent shots, if the shoulders are allowed to move back from the hips before the first shot is fired.

The body can easily adapt to relative height of cover with either high or low horizontal barricades. In the photos, tables are used for training purposes. Obviously, a conventional table offers no real cover against an armed opponent in front of you, and the tables are used for range convenience to replicate the engine compartments of automobiles or other true low cover locations.

As a rule, "artillery kneeling" will work better for relatively high horizontal cover, while "double kneeling" will be better for lower shields such as fire hydrants. We have observed in training that these two positions are like boxer shorts versus jockey shorts; if you like one, you'll hate the other. Your preference will depend on your build, muscle tone, joint structure, flexibility, etc. However, unlike underwear, there may come a time when you'll need one more than the other, and for that reason, it is wise to practice both.

For *reactive* cover, LFI recommends the Cover Crouch, which the school taught for several years as the Speed Crouch. This will bring the body down to the same height as in a high kneeling position, but you will get there faster, be able to leave to another location faster, and will not risk damaging your knees taking the position in the first place.

While kneeling is a strong position in terms of marksmanship, it is slow to get into and slow to get out of. While we practice kneeling on a comfortable shooting range, going kneeling quick in an alley full of rocks and bottles can see you getting up with one less kneecap than you started with. This is not a problem for *ensconced* cover, which is taken almost at leisure and after an assessment of the threat has shown that you probably won't need to change positions during the encounter.

To perform the Cover Crouch, you spread your feet as wide apart as they will go, flex your knees as deeply as you can, drop your backside as low as possible (ideally, to knee level), and bend forward as far as you can. There should be strong tension felt in the hamstrings. With the powerful shotgun, you will want your shooting-side leg to be to the rear, and digging into the ground with the heel to achieve the "drive leg" function a karate practitioner or boxer uses for a punch. The entire body center of gravity is lowered, and almost the whole body has become a muscular shock absorber.

One LFI student in South America was a compact, wiry police officer who had survived multiple armed encounters. However, he was frustrated that he had never been able to effectively master one of his issue weapons, the Remington 870 12-gauge pump gun. The technique he had been taught rocked him back on his heels when he fired buckshot or rifled slugs.

On the sixth of his ten days of LFI training, he learned the Cover Crouch. He was delighted to discover that the body dynamics of this technique turned his 140-pound frame into a shock absorber that, for the first time in his life, snapped his 12-gauge pump instantly back on target as soon as a shot was fired. He was so taken with the technique that he practiced it through lunch break, skipping his meal.

That evening, he was called out on a rolling stakeout of four armed robbery suspects. It was decided to pull the vehicle over. As the cars were coming to a stop, the LFI student darted from the lead police car and took a cover position behind a vehicle on the sidewalk. Because the Cover Crouch was the technique he had been practicing all day, that was the stance he assumed.

He did so none too soon. The suspects in the vehicle opened fire. The gunmen were equipped with two Smith & Wesson .38 revolvers, a Browning 9mm. Hi-Power, and a Walther .380 pistol. The LFI student immediately opened fire with his Mini-Uzi 9mm. submachinegun, emptying two full magazines in two sustained S-curve bursts. His three brother officers - armed with another Mini-Uzi, a SPAS-12 autoloading shotgun, and an 870 Remington -

joined in. Reconstruction indicated that the pitched gun battle lasted no longer than eight seconds.

The following morning, the student - the only one of the officers to have put lead into all four of the dead armed robbers - told his instructor, "Your technique works very well with Mini-Uzi."

Indeed, the Cover Crouch works well with pistol, rifle, or shotgun, and happens to be particularly suited to the reactive draw of a small handgun from an ankle holster. More to the point here, however, it is faster than kneeling when a shotgunner has to shoot from behind low cover. Its recoil absorption is so effective that one LFI graduate, Mick Sterling, uses it by choice in combat shotgun competition even when cover is not a factor, and has won numerous awards with this technique.

Even while kneeling, shoulders must be forward of hips. Rick Devoid, LFI senior instructor, demonstrates with Remington 11-87.

Double kneeling, low barricade for support. Lacking an extended magazine to use as "unipod," LFI teaches fore-end of *auto* shotgun on cover's top surface. Students should always dry-fire, as shown, before "going live."

Rationale of both double kneeling and "artillery kneeling" is seen here. In conventional kneeling position, Ayoob's shoulders have been rocked backward by 12-ga. Magnum round from Benelli 121, and he is off balance. Shell is visible above left hand.

In identical position with strong side "trailered" back in "artillery" position, muzzle lift is less (but still sharp) from Magnum 12 (shell near muzzle) but will snap back immediately since balance has been maintained. Notice also the jack-knifed forward leg with heel under pelvis.

John Shaw, center, supervises dry-fire line learning kneeling shotgun. This conventional position offers high accuracy but reduced recoil control.

Recoil of standard 12-ga. load is manageable in artillery kneeling. Tacoma PD photo.

Artillery kneeling is relatively easy to learn. Tacoma PD photo.

Resting barrel over top of horizontal cover will work with narrow cover like wall, but not wide cover like auto hood, which could deflect the slug or shot charge above the intended target.

Author demonstrates "unipod" effect of long magazine (like Choate extender on this S&W 3000 12-ga., fired southpaw) firing over auto hood. Shot charge or slug will cleanly clear the hood and fly true, *and* . . .

. . . there is minimal exposure of officer to the hostile target. (Note closed off-side eye, which while not desirable, may be necessary for some shooters when firing from non-dominant side.)

When buttocks must drop to heel in low kneeling, care must be taken to get shoulders *aggressively* forward of hips; Ayoob demonstrates with Benelli Super 90.

This sequence demonstrates redirected recoil that takes place when part of the shotgun is touching a hard surface when fired. Author takes wounded officer strong-hand only barricade position (note muzzle of Benelli Super 90 in relation to planks of picnic table that represents "cover") . . .

. . . and we see the unique dynamic. 00 Buckshot shell is ejecting from receiver; muzzle has been pushed back no more than three inches, but has driven shoulder back and around, as well as shooter's face; and muzzle remains in line with target for instantaneous followup shot. Photos courtesy Chapman Academy.

Trying to get their heads below cover, these officers use "special forces" technique and will now "roll out" with their shotguns level and ready to fire immediately. Tacoma PD photo.

Wilburn Brooker was facing manslaughter charge in Miami when he showed author how he fired his 12-gauge pump from left side window of his car at armed robber. Brooker was exonerated after an exhausting legal process; in the heat of the moment, he did not feel the pain of buttstock digging into his brachial nerve due to awkward hold with car door shielding him somewhat from .38 Special return fire. Photo courtesy Weiner, Robbins, Tunkey, & Ross, attorneys at law.

Gun expert Ed Sanow, taking an LFI-II class, demonstrates perfect low cover form using S&W m/3000 pump 12-ga. with Choate folding stock and extended magazine. The very tall Sanow has folded himself into maximum use of cover, coiling his body into the recoil, and optimizing exposure to opponent.

This officer has risen too high over the trunk of his cruiser and gone too far forward, exposing more of himself than necessary. He would also have been better protected behind the engine block of his front-wheel drive vehicle. However, sign on dumpster behind him *does* make a meaningful statement about police response to homicidal criminals. Photo courtesy Charles Remsberg.

Author takes southpaw version of Cover Crouch behind auto hood. Exposure is little more than low kneeling, but lower body is coiled for movement in any direction; recoil control is amazingly strong; and there is no risk of smashing knees on rocks seen below.

Cover Crouch can be adapted to physiology of shooter and height of cover, as seen during LFI Lethal Threat Management for Police course. Photo courtesy Tacoma PD.

Ayoob explains to students how karate "horse stance" principle was adapted to Cover Crouch.

Chapter 16

Upright Positions

Most armed engagements, pistol or long gun, involving police and armed citizens take place from the standing position. Man is an erect biped and tends to remain so in crisis, absent an opportunity for training to take over and force him into a position that might give better cover and survival potential against lethal assault.

In the StressFire system, the core technique for firing the shotgun - indeed, any "long gun" - from the standing or upright position is as follows.

Maintain a strong grasp as described previously. It is critical that the upper body be forward into the shotgun aggressively. A principle of balance is that *you will always be stronger when your shoulders are forward of your pelvis.*

To achieve this, have the left leg (if you are firing right-handed) forward of the right leg. We prefer a very aggressive stance with the forward leg far ahead of the rear one. The forward leg should be sharply flexed to take the upper body weight. Try to bring your forward arm's shoulder as close as you can to straight above the forward knee; this will help guarantee that upper body weight and mass are "into the shotgun" where they can help you recover rapidly from recoil.

The rear leg should be a "drive leg," nearly straight at the knee. The rear heel should be trying to dig into the floor or ground, helping to drive the upper body aggressively forward. This absolutely keys with the human instinct to crouch forward during the "fight or flight" response triggered by perception of maximum danger.

Avoid "standing on a tightrope," that is, with one heel right in line behind the other. This destabilizes you laterally, and recoil can turn you sharply to the side. It will also reduce your ability to track a moving target. Remember: "left foot to the left, right foot to the right."

The coiled body weight will now snap the gun back on target immediately after each shot has been fired.

To recap, the keys to the technique are:
- Gun butt in shoulder *pocket* between pectoral muscle and deltoid.
- Firing arm's elbow shoulder-high or higher.
- Thumb of firing hand on top of the tang of the receiver, pointed at target.
- Shoulders aggressively forward of hips.
- Weak leg well forward, deeply flexed.
- Keep left foot left, right foot right to create a pyramidal base, which will be much stronger than the "tightrope" stance that ensues when one heel is in line behind the other and both are in line with the gun barrel.
- Always remember to pull the gun butt tightly into the body.

Optional Additions To Technique

Claybird shooters may be surprised that no mention has yet been made of the importance of "cheeking the stock," that is, bringing the cheek down firmly onto the comb (upper edge) of the stock to keep the eye in line with the target. That technique is important when tracking a tiny, fast moving target, but not especially relevant when aiming at something that moves as slowly as a man. In addition, the much more powerful combat buckshot or slug load can transmit painful recoil to the cheek and jaws with this technique that would not be apparent with light trap or skeet loads. This will vary depending on the individual, the shape and size of their face, and the shape and size of the gunstock. If cheeking the stock works for you, do it; if it doesn't, don't worry, because you don't need that technique for combat as opposed to sporting shotgun shooting.

Many shooters will point the index finger of the forward hand toward the target when grasping the shotgun. This is common among sportshooters and hunters who often carry the practice into combat shooting, as the author does. Many feel it helps in tracking a moving target; the author finds that it lines up the long bones of the arm for more leverage when working a pump shotgun, since the rest of the arm tends to subtly follow the pointing finger. This forward hand grasp is certainly worth trying, but is not by any means a necessary component of good combat shotgun technique.

Another subtlety that is more important, especially if a pump shotgun is used, is to so position the forward arm that its elbow is pointed to the ground. This aligns skeleto-muscular support structure for the most efficient "mechanical advantage" to quickly and positively run the slide handle back and forth, and also (as any trained rifleman can confirm) applies a stronger skeletal base for holding the long gun steady on target, especially for long periods of time.

Trigger finger position has never been something shotgun instructors emphasized, perhaps because most shotgun instruction has involved claybird shooting where coarse pointing at a hyperspeed target was the issue, not careful aim at a slower human-size target. While a sporting shotgunner "slaps" the trigger, a combat shotgunner tends more to "rapidly squeeze" the trigger. If possible, placing the distal joint of the trigger finger on the trigger will give the best mechanical leverage for a controlled, straight-back pull. A running copkiller at 100 yards is a much less forgiving target for a combat shotgun loaded with rifled slugs than is a clay bird that needs only be hit by a fraction of a birdshot pattern to be considered "dead." Trigger control is, therefore, much more of a concern with the combat than the sporting shotgun.

The High Tuck Technique
One of the most efficient close-combat shotgun techniques is the High Tuck as refined and taught by Bill Groce of the Ohio Peace Officer Training Academy. It is a dramatic improvement over the previously long-taught "underarm assault position."

The body should still be aggressively forward, since the gun will still recoil and the firmly-gripping hands have attached the gun to the body. However, instead of mounting the butt of the gun at the shoulder, we now snap the comb (top edge) of the stock, not merely under the gun arm, *but all the way up until the stock touches the pectoralis tendons. IF THE STOCK IS NOT BURIED IN THE ARMPIT, THE TECHNIQUE IS NOT BEING CORRECTLY PERFORMED.*

The butt of the shotgun is now free to slide under the arm. Instead of ramming into the shoulder, the butt moves harmlessly into the open air, and recoil is taken up the the "shock absorber" of the tense, bent gun arm. The gun can be snapped into this position with extreme speed from a port arms or high ready position, and fired as soon as one feels the comb of the stock hit the axilla (armpit). Remember to bring the stock all the way up; we tell our students that the stock had better smell like Right Guard when we get the gun back.

This lines up the gun barrel level with the shooter's chest, which will be level with an opponent's torso assuming even ground. If the butt is low under the armpit instead of high up and touching, the shot will go high, and toward the shooter's weak side; i.e., at seven yards, the shooter will fire over the suspect's right shoulder if the comb of the stock is not in place. Some students will additionally need to lock the weak arm straight out to guarantee a level gun muzzle. This is situational and dependent on the build of the given shooter.

The thumb of the firing hand MUST be locked down tight and hard, and the middle finger kept well back away from the trigger guard, when using this technique! If not, since the stock is no longer buttressed against the shoulder but instead is recoiling freely toward the rear, the trigger guard can be driven painfully against the middle finger. I saw one individual break his middle finger with eight fast shots from a Benelli when he deliberately refused to use the proper grasp. With the thumb locked down and maximum hand strength applied, the hand will move with the gun; if the hand relaxes, or if the thumb goes up as it would with a from-the-shoulder technique, the gunstock will slide through the now-weakened hand and the impact of the trigger guard to the middle finger will result.

The High Tuck is inherently a short range technique. It is geared to working at a distance the width of an average bedroom. This is all to the good, since this is where the home defense shotgun will generally be employed, and the technique is free of painful recoil when done properly. However, since the line of the gun's barrel is now lower than the line of sight, by a significant margin, the shot blast will tend to go high much beyond a few steps away.

This can be dealt with through practice. One female officer who learned this technique was able to qualify with the High Tuck, using rifled slugs, at a range of 25 yards. She had to, since her shoulder had been dislocated through bad techniques taught by her police department. However, it takes a rare level of commitment and repetitious training to make the High Tuck effective much beyond seven yards.

It is also important to note that fleshy people might find a bit of their arm's skin getting abraded by the shotgun butt if it is not all the way past the arm. We have also noted that the rolled-up sleeves of some military uniforms will tend to catch the stock when the gun is fired in this manner. We have not, however, noticed that any of the Remington or Choate folding stocks cause any unusual problem when compared to conventional stocks when fired from the high tuck. Pistol-grip assault stocks make for a particularly strong shooting stance with this technique, since the locked wrist can apply forward pressure and the arm is better positioned for dynamic muscle tension to turn the limb into a shock absorber.

Within its range, this technique can be used for kneeling positions as well as standing. It is not necessarily suited for the Cover Crouch technique that will be shown later, however, because the torse will be bent more forward from there and shots may go low. On the other hand, if you find yourself shooting high with the High Tuck from a conventional standing position, combining it with the Cover Crouch may act as a correction.

Pec-Vest

The Pectoral Vest position is another recoil-reducing shotgun technique developed by Bill Groce, and is yet another excellent reason why any Good Guy going in harm's way should be wearing a ballistic vest. When this technique is used, recoil is absorbed by layers of nerveless, unfeeling Kevlar, the armid fiber that was developed by DuPont to replace steel in belted radial tires, and is five times tougher than steel in tensile strength.

With the Kevlar ballistic vest in place, the gun butt is placed in line with the nipple against the pectoral muscle, between the nipple and the collarbone. On the female, it must be placed *above* the soft tissue of the breast.

Since the shooter is now going to take a hard impact on that pectoral muscle, he or she should tighten and harden that muscle accordingly. It is now more effective to bend the shooting arm's elbow *down,* with the joint pointed to the ground, as the butt is firmly pulled into the pectoral muscle through the vest.

The gun muzzle is now higher into the cone of tunnel vision than it was in the high tuck, and therefore, this technique better survives stress. As with other techniques, shoulders should be forward of hips.

One can look over the barrel with the StressPoint Index technique described elsewhere, or lower the head all the way forward and all the way down (imagine doing a vulture imitation) and the eye can take a conventional sight picture. This allows the Pec-Vest technique to be used at any distance within the range of the weapon and load being employed.

With the Pec-Vest technique, *the chest should be turned more square to the target than the body-bladed stance most target shooters use with a long gun.* This will prevent the gun butt from skidding off the vest. It will also prevent, or at least minimize, exposure of the weak-side armpit area (not protected by Kevlar) to the incoming small arms fire of the opponent. The Pec-Vest technique also eliminates one problem with the regular shoulder pocket stance, which is that the vest may cover the shoulder pocket and cause the gun butt to skid off painfully into the brachial plexus between deltoid and bicep.

Since the gun arm can more efficiently be held with the elbow pointed down instead of up and out, there may arguably be somewhat less arm exposure when firing from behind vertical cover, such as around the corner of a building.

The Pec-Vest is the preferred technique with most autoloading shotguns over the High Tuck. This is because most autoloading shotguns require the butt to be held rigidly against a support surface, such as the shoulder, so the spring-loaded bolt can work efficiently inside the frame. When the frame is moving backward with the whole gun, the dynamic that controls recoil with the High Tuck, the bolt can run out of momentum before completing its task and thus jam the shotgun. The Browning-type long recoil semiautomatic shotgun seems the least susceptible to this problem. If one must fire a Benelli or a gas-operated shotgun from the High Tuck, an effort should be made for the bicep to lock the flat of the stock hard against the body, as if one was applying a headlock.

The Pec-Vest technique can be used with vertical or horizontal cover, and from standing or kneeling positions, very effectively.

Two students, same double-powered gun, two instructors with cat-eating canary smiles but for different reasons.

Ben Mozrall, NH State Police, catches a student who might otherwise have gone on his back after single-loaded shot from Ithaca Roadblocker Mag-10. Note not only elevation of muzzle, but entire body of male police academy student rocked backward by recoil. Photo courtesy *Law and Order* magazine.

Author looks on approvingly as LFI-II student Barbara Budnar fires her first shot from Mag-10, same 3 1/2" Magnum #4 load. Note that muzzle has not left target, and Budnar is in position to sustain rapid fire, which is exactly what she is about to do despite unleashing a shell equivalent to two 12-gauge buckshot rounds at once. Photo by Marty Hayes.

Frank Muggianu photographed Ayoob doing this triple tap from "kaizin-dache" stance. Rear leg is drive leg, shoulders began aggressively forward of hips, body weight strongly onto bent forward leg. 3 rounds of full-power 12-gauge have been fired in one second, two spend hulls flying toward camera and the third cycling the action. Shots took out pelvis, solar plexus, and head of target. Gun is LaRocca Custom Remington 1100 12-gauge Magnum.

Size and mass are definite advantages in rapid 12-gauge fire. Here at Second Chance, the lightest man (author) uses .45 pistol with compensator, while bigger partners work 12-ga. pump and auto on 3-man team.

Same aggressive kaizin-dache stance works well with full auto fire, as Ayoob demonstrates with Uzi submachinegun on sustained burst, Bob Houzenga timing.

Even with shoulders slightly forward, recoil control can be well maintained. Here Ayoob's Benelli m/121, sans recoil reducers, is still on target with 00 Express Buck shell flying past muzzle after alighting from van at Missouri State Championship. Chapman Academy Photo.

Even the sharp recoil of 12-gauge Magnum is manageable from kaizin-dache stance. Gun is Benelli m/121 in rapid fire.

Author demonstrates Pec-Vest for Canadian police instructors, using Remington 870 12-gauge pump. He is looking over barrel with StressPoint Index.

Good big man will generally beat a good small man with equivalent 12-ga. shotguns, author has found. He and LFI-trained Bill Grimmett start in nearly identical positions with 12-gauge pumps . . .

. . . but as each fire first shot, 160-lb. Ayoob is driven back proportionally farther than 280-lb. Grimmett. Both, however, are still on target for simultaneous second shot; difference will show up more dramatically as string of fire lengthens to targets #3, #4, etc.

Author snugs butt of Benelli into shoulder strap area of Second Chance vest on gun hand side. Note that torso is square to target, not angled. Gun can actually be fired effectively from here one-handed.

Support hand comes forward, arm locked, shoulders aggressively forward of hips. Looking over top of gun, shooter can fire very effectively to a surprising distance while focusing on target, with gunsight in peripheral vision using "Stresspoint Index" explained in original "StressFire" text.

By bringing head forward and down like a vulture, shooter can take a correct sight picture and fire fast and accurate without pain to as far as the accuracy of a 12-gauge rifled slug will take him. A female officer must be careful to have gun butt above, not on, the breast.

Seen from side, Pec-Vest stance is combined with "vulture" technique, head forward and down. This not only allows perfect sight picture with pain-free recoil, but forces upper body weight forward and into the gun for maximum rapid-fire control.

Cops should do at least part of their firearms training in uniform to see if any constraints of body dynamics might be present "on the job" that wouldn't show up in range wear. Author fires dept.-issue Benelli Super-90 from Pec-Vest with StressPoint sight index. Badges and nameplates should be removed during this: they will be bent out of shape when crushed between gun butt and ballistic vest.

135

Chapter 17

Standing Barricade

Oddly enough, very little conventional combat shotgun training is done from behind cover. This is surprising, since the shotgun is normally deployed only when there is warning of extreme, deadly danger, which is precisely the sort of situation that should make one more aware of cover than ever.

We shall begin with vertical cover, for instance, the edge of a building. One needs to violate standard balance principles here, since to have left foot left and right foot right would put one leg and part of the upper body outside cover and in the field of opposing fire. One must consciously draw the rear foot inside the line of the area protected by the cover. This makes it all the more important that the hips be further back from the barricade than the shoulders to guarantee recoil control.

With a light recoiling weapon, like a .223 rifle or a pistol-caliber carbine, any number of barricade positions adapted from pistol shooting will work. With the much more powerful shotgun, however, the forward hand should firmly grip the stock.

To minimize body exposure and maximize control, it is important to *place the edge of the barrel against the barricade.* Contrary to popular belief, this will not ruin accuracy or alter point of aim/point of impact with rifled slug or with buckshot; it will actually improve per-shot hit potential. The contact point should be well behind the muzzle (so the barrel does not come inward and back off the barricade upon recoil) but well ahead of a pump gun's slide handle, so recharging for the followup shots will not be impeded. In short, the contact point is halfway between the front of the slide handle and the muzzle. With an autoloading shotgun, contact point can be on the fore-end of the weapon.

It has been theorized that the barrel could be bent against the barricade. It is conceivable that if the barrel were forcibly *smashed* against a very hard edge to achieve this position, a very slight dent could be made in the barrel, but the author has never seen it happen in the course of extensive training. Even if it did, the shotgun barrels are far cheaper than human lives.

What *will* happen whenever any part of the shotgun touches a hard surface is that recoil will be redirected. Instead of the gun kicking upward as it might have before, recoil movement will be almost entirely straight back. The good news is that the sights will come more rapidly back on target for followup shots; the bad news is that the shooter can be more readily knocked backwards if not in a position of solid balance. In any case, the felt impact of the recoil will be greater. Fortunately, when fight or flight reflex takes place, the body tends to coil itself more aggressively forward (in this case, better bracing itself for well-balanced recoil absorption) and norepinephrine release will make the body much more resistant to pain. Kick that was uncomfortable in training will go unfelt in time of stress, though soreness may be palpable after the encounter is over.

When firing from the left side of the wall if right handed, or vice-versa, it is imperative that the gun be fired from the weak-side shoulder. In pistol shooting, the Jim Cirillo technique developed circa 1980 allowed one to fire around a weak-side barricade by simply turning the gun over 45° without unduly sacrificing exposure to the opponent. No analogous technique exists with the long gun.

Famed shotgun competitor John Satterwhite developed a match technique in which the shooter kept the gun at the strong shoulder and fired around the weak side by coming up on the ball of the strong foot and leaning out from cover. Though precariously balanced when firing full power ammo, it worked well with light trap and skeet loads. However, the targets did not shoot back, which is well because this technique forced the entire head and much of the upper body out into the field of opposing fire, effectively voiding the advantage of the shooter's cover.

Weak-side barricade with the shotgun or other long guns is best done, then, as a mirror image of strong side technique, fired from the weak side shoulder. The person with a very dominant eye on the strong side may have to condition himself or herself to close that eye when firing from the opposite shoulder to force the remaining eye to access the gunsights.

To perform this technique, the shooter needs to learn the *hand change.* In training, the gun should be on safe when switching stances, though in combat there may not be time for this; therefore, at all times, one must be conditioned to have the finger outside the trigger guard except when actually, intentionally firing.

To go from strong side to weak side, the hand change is best executed as follows:

1. Put gun on safe.
2. Bring rear hand up to fore-end, behind forward hand.
3. Bring forward hand back to firing position, simultaneously stepping back with the leg that had been forward until it is now to the rear.
4. Take mirror image of your previous firing stance, release safety, and commence firing as necessary.

Note that rear hand comes forward and then forward hand comes back; this is done to keep the gun under firm, balanced control. When the forward hand comes back first, the muzzle will dip and the shooter may lose control of the weapon.

When the weak hand operates the typical crossbolt safety catch located on the trigger guard, technique is as follows. If the button is at the *rear* of the trigger guard (Remington, Ithaca, Benelli) the left hand's *middle* finger presses in right to left to put the safety catch on "fire", while the *index* finger is generally better positioned to press out, left to right, to put the catch on "safe." Similarly, for the right handed shooter, the index finger can better press out for "safe" when the gun is mounted to the right, assuming a factory-produced weapon geared for the right handed shooter.

The index finger, being farther forward, will generally work better for moving the safety crossbolt in either direction when the safety is mounted on the *front* of the trigger guard, as with a Winchester or Hi-Standard shotgun. The top-tang safety of the Mossberg, Savage/Stevens, or older Smith & Wesson 916 series pump shotgun, being thumb-actuated, is functionally ambidextrous, as is that of the typical double barrel shotgun whether the barrels are mounted over/under or side by side.

Dominant side standing barricade: 12-ga. pump has barrel against wall midway between muzzle and slide handle; shoulders are forward; cover-side leg is straight back, behind cover and agressively behind hips.

On left side barricade, one should fire from left shoulder; it can even be done with Mossberg Bullpup, though not recommended, if care is taken to keep face clear of shell ejection.

Ayoob fires wounded officer style, left hand only. Note barrel against barricade redirecting the recoil.

Shot is fired. Because shoulder was not forward enough, muzzle has lifted somewhat, but most of the movement has been straight back, with barrel's contact with barricade redirecting the recoil.

For comparison, using the same Benelli Super 90, same 00 Buck, and *two*-hand hold, but *away* from the barricade, muzzle jump is nearly the same. With body more forward recoil would be less, but this is not always possible with awkward barricade positions, especially when firing one-handed. Photos courtesy Chapman Academy.

Right-handed shooter on left barricade with Benelli 121 and rifled slugs. Note that sharp recoil has drive shoulders backward, but body is still coiled to snap forward again, barrel remains in contact with barricade, and sights remain in line with the downrange threat.

If three or pole is the *real* cover instead of just a replication of the corner of a bullet-resistant wall, consider this "wraparound, belly to barricade" position if you can still work the gun. As illustration shows, opponent will have to move much farther to outflank you for a vital hit, offsetting your exposure of forward arm.

Same vertical cover positions work well with carbines, like HK 94 9 mm. shown, or submachineguns, rifles, etc.

On left-side wall, switching to left hand with long gun is only viable position to maintain effective cover. Ben Mozrall demonstrates with folding-stock Remington 870. Photo courtesy of *Law and Order* magazine.

Should gun arm be up in best marksman position, or down? Look from target eye view and see for yourself. On left barricade, author's only significant exposure is firing arm when arm is up for best rapid-fire accuracy and control.

WIth arm down, arm is *still* in field of opposing fire, but control that could have suppressed that incoling has been sacrificed. Note also slightly more torso exposure: "arm up" position tends to pull torso back in behind cover.

Chapter 18

Specialized Techniques

StressFire Star

The good news about cover is that is stops bullets; the bad news is that it isolates you in one position and contributes to tunnel vision that goes forward toward the threat that forced you to take cover initially. This makes you vulnerable to being outflanked.

In the early days of the StressFire system, we recognized this problem and adapted an Aikido movement technique we call the StressFire Star, which allows you to pivot to any point of a 360° star from kneeling. Finalized in 1980, it appeared in the 1983 textbook "StressFire," and when the US Army adopted StressFire it appeared in turn in their Combat Pistol manual FM23-35. It works well with a shotgun, as Brian Felter noted in his 1991 text on the subject.

As the photos show, one simply pivots toward the angle of attack by turning the upper body toward the weak side, raising the pelvis higher off the ground to get more latitude. When turning toward the strong side, bring the upright knee down as soon as the body binds and fire from double kneeling. Continuing to turn, if the body binds again, bring the other knee up. This allows full rotation.

Note that you may find yourself firing with left knee down and right knee up but gun to right shoulder (or, at left shoulder, with right knee down and left knee up). This interferes with body dynamics to the extent that one must consciously and intently bring the shoulder forward of the hips when firing, or in recoil the gun will gain leverage, slowing time between shots and even knocking the shooter backward.

Toe to Shoulder

Smith & Wesson Academy popularized a technique in which the bottom edge ("toe") of the shotgun butt touches the shoulder instead of the full buttplate. This brings the comb of the stock higher, giving some faster sight acquisition and "cheeking." Those who have tried it are widely mixed in their reactions.

Some find that they perceive less kick since less of the gun is touching them. Others find that the smaller contact point concentrates recoil and makes it sharper. This is highly individual. The author has noted that the smaller contact surface makes it easier to get a poor mount to the shoulder in a hasty reaction situation and does not care for it.

"Toe to Shoulder" is not so much a technique in and of itself as a variant of core shotgun grasp. Developed from skeet shooting, many will find it better suited for light sporting birdshot loads than for heavy combat ammo. Also, because it tends to straighten the head up and because "where the head goes, the body follows," it makes it more difficult to keep the shoulders aggressively forward for sustained rapid-fire recoil control with combat loads.

Like any variant technique, the individual should try it under supervision in realistic training to see if it is worth adding to his or her personal repertoire.

Front Snap

Another technique promulgated by Bill Groce is to thrust the gun forward like a bayonet stroke and fire as the forward arm "hits the end of its tether." It can be effective and lightning fast at close range. The bent dominant arm absorbs recoil well.

Downsides to this Front Snap include the fact that it takes a good deal of practice to be able to hit with it beyond very close range, since as with a pistol grip shotgun, index is largely lost. Also, a very firm grip is required by the forward hand especially and if the rear hand lets loose, the gun can come back. For this reason, the butt should never be in line with the face.

While not the author's favorite technique, it is street proven. I interviewed an Ohio policeman who credited the Front Snap with saving his life. Rounding a building corner during a manhunt, he was confronted with an armed suspect, whose gun was levelled on the cop. As he threw himself back out of the way, the cop reflexively unleashed a round of 00 buck with a Front Snap, striking and instantly neutralizing the suspect.

Chapter 19

Malfunctions: Prevention, Reduction, Response

Everything produced by Man, including our parents' children, can screw up occasionally. This is perhaps more true for the combat shotgun than for some other weapons, for a number of reasons.

First, the commonly-used slide action shotgun is heir to human error. It takes an uncommonly cool hand, even among the ranks of seasoned pump gunners, to bring the pump sharply *all* the way back and *all* the way forward when fight or flight reflex has hit its peak, and one's body is trying to simultaneously duck behind cover and return fire. The situation gets even worse when the person behind the gun has not been conditioned to operate a pump gun as second nature.

Consider the following observation from "You Can't Miss," the combat competition manual written by the famous three-gun shooting champion, John Shaw:

> What makes combat shotgunning different from any other use of the scattergun is the emphasis on hitting multiple targets in a short time span. This is a skill that even most police departments overlook. I once trained an elite SWAT team in handgunning, and after a tough day of pistol shooting, we turned to their issue pump shotguns. They'd all been bragging about how good the team was with shotguns, so I put up five targets at 15 yards, about one yard apart. The drill was to put one slug in each target in five seconds - not a very tough drill, actually. Of the seven members of the team, only one member made it through without short stroking his pump with all hits on the target. My time on the drill, using one of their terrible Winchester

1200 pumps, was 3.25 seconds with all hits in the nine-ring. Two cases of slugs later, most of the team could do it, too.[1]

If you keep a pump shotgun for defense, remember that the pump must be worked all the way. A short stroke can lock the pump action up, leaving the shotgun useless.

Relatively few readers of this book will have a couple of cases of 12-ga. shotgun slugs to put through their pump guns under expert tutelage. The simple fact is that, if economics allow it, purchasing a top-quality autoloading shotgun to begin with shortcuts the danger of the short-stroke, and cuts out one major area of shotgun malfunction entirely.

Keep your shotgun clean. Carbon builds up inside the gun from firing. Dust, dirt and grit from the environment of the weapon can build up inside, sometimes exacerbated by overly heavy oiling that creates a suspension medium to hold crud in place and help it coalesce into a gooey mess. Poorly manufactured shotshells can leak plastic granules into the mechanism. All these things can and will result in jammed shotguns.

Autoloading shotguns, the gas operated ones in particular, will be prone to malfunction when they become dirty. It is critical for any safety-rescue equipment to be sparkling clean and properly lubricated when it is stored with the assumption that it may have to be deployed at any moment to protect innocent life. Take a cue from your local fire department: keep your equipment sparkling clean and ready to roll at all times as if your life depended on it. The reason is, if you need to use the instrument for its intended purpose, your life *will* depend on it.

Use appropriate ammunition. As you will quickly learn in any basic hunter safety course, a 20-gauge shotgun shell inserted into a 12-gauge shotgun will slide into the chamber and stop partway down the barrel. A 12-gauge shell can now be loaded into the chamber and fired. When that happens, the 20-ga. shell part way down the barrel will explode, blowing your forward hand into granulated protoplasm. That is the most obvious aspect.

Shotgun shells come in different lengths. Many if not most 12-gauge shotguns will feed only a 2 3/4" shell, though some weapons are chambered for the 3" Magnum round. 12-gauge shells of any length won't feed in each other's firing chambers, but treacherously, they'll all load into the magazine under the barrel.

At one Idaho police department, the auxiliary police decided to clean the department's shotguns. Appalled at the condition of the old shotgun shells, the citizen-cops paid out of their own pockets to buy new ammo. With the best of all possible intentions, they went to the gunshop and ordered the most powerful 12-gauge buckshot in the store. Obligingly, the dealer served them up with 3" 12-gauge Magnum 00 buckshot. These shells slid smoothly into the magazine of the agency-issued Remington 870s, which unfortunately, had chambers cut for standard 2 3/4" shells.

The night came when an offender disarmed an officer of that department, and shot him through the torso with his own .357 Magnum service revolver. The wounded cop ran around the car, trying to get to the only other gun accessible, the cruiser shotgun. He pumped the action, but it stuck; the three-inch shell would not enter the 2 3/4" chamber.

The man with the stolen gun was closing in, raising the .357 for the coup de grace. The young officer showed us what fight or flight reflex is all about: he closed the shotgun's action with enormous force and pulled the trigger.

The 15 00 pellets that emerged from the gun muzzle slew the would-be copkiller outright, and the gun jammed up solid as the plastic shell case fire-formed past the chamber, but it was no longer a matter of consequence. The officer recovered from his wound and returned to duty.

It should be noted that this writer has seen students run a few rounds of 3" Magnum through their 2 3/4" shotguns before figuring out why the gun was so hard to pump. It can be done, but it is also on the list of Things You Don't Want To Happen In A Gunfight.

Inspect Your Shells Before Loading. Remember what we said about no one being perfect? This author's extensive experience with combat shotgun ammo indicates that no brand has better quality control than Winchester, yet you note the photograph of a Winchester shell that came from the box with defective brass. It was fortunately discovered on the training range before it could be loaded into a weapon. Just to see what would happen, it was inserted into a shotgun, and sure enough, it was jam-o-matic time.

Various manufacturers have had various lots of ammo that were not ideal. Some were not crimped right, and plastic pellet-buffering granules escaped into the mechanism of the shotgun. In sufficient quantity, these can jam a shotgun by themselves; it gets worse when hot in-car temperatures melt the plastic into a sludgy white mass. This can happen inside the gun, especially when the shells are in the metal tube magazine of a shotgun that is racked upright on a dashboard in front of a glass windshield. The glass intensifies the sunlight, the steel conducts and holds the heat, and the magazine tube reaches about the temperature of the upper levels of Hell, which is where one who has been sufficiently indiscreet can wind up if they try to use such a maltreated shotgun to protect their life.

In addition, spring tension in magazine tubes can distort the normally straight walls of a buckshot-loaded cartridge sufficiently that the shell becomes "out of round" and will no longer cycle into the firing chamber. When the shell has been pumped in and out of the gun multiple times by people who don't know how to use magazine shell-release trippers to unload shotguns, the rims of the shells can be chewed up sufficiently by the extractor that a jam can result when the round has to cycle through the mechanism "for real."

Malfunction Reduction

We used to call it jam clearing. In the late 1980s, when police instructors who had been telling their students that revolvers were reliable and auto pistols jammed suddenly had to make their men confident with autoloaders, the term "malfunction reduction" came into vogue.

Cops have strange semantics. They speak of "minimum qualification" as if it was somehow desirable instead of mediocre...they teach each other to say "I performed a technique" instead of saying "I hit him," as if this will somehow make the necessary use of force seem kinder and gentler...and they speak of "reducing a stoppage" as if that would somehow make the cop feel more confident than being able to clear a jam.

The single most common shotgun malfunction observed in combat training is the perhaps misnamed "double feed." This is the situation in which the bolt is closed on the chamber and a shell slips its stop(s) from the magazine and is propelled under the bolt, caught between it and the shell lift. This causes sufficient friction pressure in most weapons that the bolt cannot come back after the first shot is fired to cycle the gun for the second shot.

Various techniques have been taught to clear this malfunction, none of which are immediately and reliably effective. One was to keep the muzzle on an angle away from one's face and, holding the slide release lever back if necessary, apply rearward tension to the slide handle while ramming the toe of the stock firmly into the ground. This simultaneously applied enormous pressure backward against the bolt, while hopefully delivering sufficient inertial force to drive the jammed shell forward enough into the magazine for the bolt above it to cycle. It worked plus/minus half the time, depending on how many rounds were in the magazine and how much spring tension was therefore holding the recalcitrant shell in place beneath the bolt.

The other technique was to use a key or, God help us, the tip of a knife blade, to drive the trapped shell forward and back into the magazine. Some misguided shooters suggested cutting a slot into the shell lift to expedite this, and the theory gained sufficient credence in gullible gun-related magazines that not only did gunsmiths start offering the alteration, but such respected manufacturers as Franchi and Benelli integrated it into their designs.

We pause briefly to consider a simple fact. The primer of the shotgun shell is located at its center. A key or knife-point pushed up through a slot in the follower against the shell will contact the primer. Done forcibly — and forcible impact *is* what causes a primer to fire a round — the shell can go off.

The shell is at this moment in line behind another whole magazine of shells. When the rear one goes, all the ones in front of it will go off in a chain discharge. This happens at a moment when both hands are in the vicinity of these shells, and one's face is looking down into the magazine area.

The result of this chain detonation is likely to blow both your hands to jellied protoplasm, burst both your eardrums, evacuate your eyesockets, and turn your face into something resembling a Halloween mask that was dropped into a meat grinder. When you wake up in the hospital you are likely to be a deaf, blind mute who no longer even has hands to kill himself with.

Those who bought into this theory and recognized what was wrong with it after the LFI 1985 "Advanced Combat Shotgun" video that made the above statement, then modified their position. Why, they said, just run the knife blade up through the *edge* of the frame where it would only hit the *edge* of the shell rim.

Uh...yeah. Right. And, as they also noted, "be careful not to touch the primer."

This is a good time to go to the next stage of the discussion, which is based on the street instead of the range: you need a gun to shoot back with, your shotgun won't work anymore, so what do you *do?*

Malfunction Response

When your shotgun seizes up, don't sit there trying to fix it. Dump it. *Lose* it. DROP that useless piece of jammed equipment and go immediately to the loaded and ready handgun that almost all combat shotgun users will have on their person in any situation in which they will have picked up a shotgun.

"Wait a minute," say the people who want to run knife points against shotgun primers. "What if you grabbed the gun from you bedside during a home invasion, and you sleep nude, and that shotgun is all you *have?!?* Where are you going to get a pistol?"

Well, to tell you the truth, you'll get the pistol the same damn place you got the screwdriver and the knife and the keys.

The police officer will have a pistol on their person. The homeowner will also have one at hand, unless he has had a major planning failure. In home defense, the shotgun is not the primary weapon; the handgun is, because the handgun allows the householder to move with one hand or (assuming a holster) both hands free - to call the cops, to work the light switches, to rush the kids into the safe room, and whatnot. The shotgun is a *fallback* weapon.

We reiterate. If the shotgun jams, go to the pistol. You may wish to put the shotgun in the weak hand and fire strong-handed-only with the pistol; many credentialed experts absolutely refuse to leave a firearm behind where the Bad Guys can get at it.

This writer feels differently. If he is holding a pump gun with a shell firmly jammed between bolt and shell lift, he will throw the weapon *at* the opponent, on the theory that there are few better weapons for the opponent to be armed with than a jammed one that will require gunsmith tools to make operate again. It is most unlikely that you will be involved in a shootout against a fully-equipped graduate of the Remington Armorer's School.

If the gun must be left behind, one officer survival expert notes that the Remington and Ithaca pump shotgun can be easily and quickly disassembled: take the barrel with you, and no one will ever kill anyone with just the parts you left behind.

Another school of thought suggests that, if it's possible, you sink the muzzle of your jammed shotgun as deep as you can into mud or snow and *then* leave it behind: the person who pulls the trigger will have a most unpleasant surprise when they pull the trigger and the back pressure blows the gun, assuming they can get a shootable round into the firing chamber.

Standard remedy for double-feed malfunction is to ram to of stock into ground while driving slide handle backward, keeping muzzle clear of head. Here, it works for Ayoob during LFI-II class with Remington 870 LT-20 . . . but the technique is not always effective.

Brian Felter, left-handed author of "Police Shotguns and Carbines," demonstrates proper response when shotgun ceases to shoot: draw pistol and sustain fire. Here, Brian is holding Beretta 1200 with his weak hand, Beretta 92 with the strong; dumping shotgun for two-hand pistol hold is also viable.

Always inspect ammo before loading; this factory-fresh round of Winchester/Western 00 Buckshot, famous for its quality control, came from the box with this split case head, totally jamming the weapon when, after discovery, it was tried on the firing line.

What's wrong with this picture? Winchester 1200's bolt is back and open, but slide handle forward. One part had come loose, "killing" the gun; always inspect the shotgun before storing it ready for defensive use.

Work your shotgun extensively in training, so problems show up safely there, instead of on the street. This LFI student examines shells that failed to fire in his drum magazine assault shotgun . . .

. . . and realizes that light primer hits, off center because drum didn't bring shells into proper alignment, caused the misfires.

Don't be 'the first on your block" to see if a new design works. This USAS-12 "assault shotgun" is shown jammed with the factory-recommended ammo.

Inspection shows cause of USAS-12 jam. With relatively few rounds fired, contact surfaces of steel parts are peening out of shape at critical points. Author cannot recommend this weapon at this writing.

Ayoob demonstrates his idea of proper shotgun malfunction response. Jammed gun is dropped into weeds, and defender ducks behind large rock, having drawn sidearm to agressively continue to fight for survival.

As explained in text, author feels widely taught technique of running key through slit in shell lifter to clear jam is extremely dangerous.

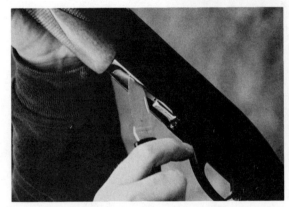

Using knife around outside edge of shell lift to clear jammed shell is only slightly less stupid, slow, and dangerous as running something through a slot in the middle of the lift. Author forbids this technique in his training.

Chapter 20

Shotgun Techniques That Work When Wounded

The shotgun is broken out for high risk missions, and high risk means a greater likelihood of being wounded or disabled, yet few people put that together and train wounded officer techniques with the combat shotgun. LFI has done so since early in the 1980s.

If lower mobility is lost, the shotgun can be fired from one's back. A Kentucky state trooper used this position to shotgun to death the man who had paralyzed him with .223 fire. It should be practiced at least dry fire. It is tricky in live fire practice, however, since powerful recoil jamming the shoulder against the hard ground can cause a training injury.

Wounded people often double over or black out for an instant, and can wind up on both knees either way. This is another good reason to practice the double kneeling position shown in the low cover chapter.

If the use of one arm is lost, any shotgun can be fired at least once from the "good arm side" shoulder one handed, and an auto shotgun can be fired from there repeatedly; it is another of the autoloading shotgun's advantages. A pistol-grip assault stock works much better from the shoulder in one-handed fire, though a conventional stock *can* work from there.

The elbow should be pointed *down* to give the shooter more skeletomuscular leverage to pull the gun in tight, controlling recoil and stabilizing aim. The shoulder should still be forward, with the opposite leg forward and taking the body weight. If the shoulder cannot be used due to lack of strength, the comb of the stock can be tucked under the armpit like a one-handed high tuck. Here again, the assault stock will work better since the wrist can be locked for greater strength.

To prevent an accidental second shot if the beginning shooter slips after recoil, the author STRONGLY suggests that this technique be learned with the gun loaded with only one shot at a time to start. Supervision should always include one instructor for each pupil.

Begin with the student aimed two-handed on target. Point gun arm elbow down and pull stock in tight. Drop forward hand away. Fire. On Safe. Reload and repeat. Then do the same with the other arm. The student will be surprised to learn how quickly the one-handed 12-gauge can be mastered.

We prefer to use assault-stocked shotguns for this training for all students. This is because the bending of the wrist required for this technique with a conventional stock could theoretically injure a shooter with weak wrists, and will in any case be slightly painful. It will, however, be less painful than getting shot with a coup de grace because, once wounded, the student didn't know what to do with a two-handed weapon when only one hand was left.

There are a couple of ways to operate the slide pump shotgun one handed, none of them safe. The method used by Edmundo Mireles in the Miami shootout was to put the butt of his 870 on the pavement where he sat with his back against the side of a car, clamping the gun steady between the thighs, and jacking the pump with his good hand. The gun can be "flipped" (the technique used by Linda Hamilton in "Terminator 2" and shown in the 1984 LFI training video, "Wounded Officer Return Fire Techniques") but because of the way the gun muzzle swings around, we consider it too dangerous for live fire training.

Working one-handed with a slide action shotgun will give one a new appreciation for the semiautomatic smoothbore. The confident, highly trained handgunner should determine in training whether it might make more sense for him or her to go immediately to the one-handed gun, their sidearm, and set aside the long gun if one of their arms is taken out by play by opposing fire.

To reload one-handed, get down on one knee (the knee on the good hand side) with the other knee up. Lay the shotgun into the juncture of hip and thigh of the wounded-side leg, its butt against the down knee of the good-side leg. This will give the gun maximum stability as you use your one remaining hand to insert shells into the chamber and then the magazine.

One-handed shooter can brace auto shotgun over low cover using fore-end . . .

. . . or pump *or* auto using extended magazine as "unipod" support. In previous photo Ayoob is double kneeling, while LFI students in this picture use the "artillery kneeling" position

One-hand armtuck works well only with pistol-gripped shotgun like this Benelli Super 90.

Variants on right-hand-only theme. 1st (foreground) shooter is firing from Pec-Vest position, muzzle has lifted somewhat; lady 2nd in did not lock in hard enough, and is experiencing exaggerated recoil (note shell passing her wrist); 3rd shooter has been forced nearly out of picture by recoil of his Remington 870, whose slide has unlocked itself from kick; farthest shooter is in excellent control of his SPAS 12 as he fires his last shot.

Conventional-stock shotgun can also be fired one-handed from regular shoulder position if not high tuck, with or without barricade support. This is standard-stock Benelli Super 90.

Author fires Benelli Super 90 from standing barricade, weak hand only. Note obvious advantage of autoloading shotgun in this scenario.

With one arm down, this would be one-hand reload. Drop to knee on same side as working arm, other knee bent upward. Brace shotgun across that leg at juncture of thigh and hip, butt on ground. Free hand can now load both magazine (shown) and chamber.

Chapter 21

Combat Shotgun Competition

Competition in shooting builds familiarity, confidence, and skill. This is why forward thinking police departments that issue their officers take-home cars complete with cruiser shotguns have encouraged them to use those guns for hunting and other sport shooting.

However, some shotgun "games" are more useful for this than others. Hunting, with the gun constantly in hand, does more than anything else encourage familiarity and accustom you to the feel of the weapon in your hand.

Clay bird shooting builds familiarity, but has some shortcomings. First, light loads are used; the concept of shooting with light loads but carrying heavy ones has been recognized as antithetical to combat weapons training for decades. Moreover, the flying bird flies faster than a man can move, and can condition you to over-lead and missing a running, dangerous human adversary. "When you start seeing small, flying criminals, you want someone to take your shotgun *away* from you."

IPSC, the International Practical Shooting Confederation, is sponsoring more and more shotgun competitions. In many areas, practice is limited to birdshot, but you can use high-base field loads to equal the recoil characteristics of a true combat load. A good IPSC course will encompass rapid movement, speed reloading, and multiple targets. For information on a club near you engaged in this sort of organized shooting, write the US Practical Shooting Association (USPSA, the American arm of IPSC) at P.O. Box 811,

163

Sedro Wooley, WA 98284.

Bowling pin shooting, inaugurated by Richard Davis in the mid 1970s, has caught on at a local level nationwide. Most outdoor clubs have at least some shotgun events. There's little in the way of tactics: simply strafe down the pins as fast as you can. What it *will* do is force you to use a full power load, and build your confidence in just how rapidly you can do so if you employ the techniques in this book. Pins are reaction targets; you will subconsciously want to see what happens. Man is the ultimate reaction target. If you focus too long on Suspect A to see what happens to him after the shot, you've given Suspect B time to shoot you. Pin shooting under match pressure conditions you to subconsciously recognize when you've done it right and the shot has been good, allowing you to *instantly* track the weapon to the next target.

In this sort of competition, you discover such subtleties as the fact that a shotgun held to your right shoulder will kick to the right, making it slightly easier to shoot left target/right target than vice versa. This can be a life saver in a multiple threat situation in which all opponents are equally dangerous. In training, however, half your shooting should be right to left, half left to right, since you never know which side will be occupied by the most dangerous opponent, who must be shot first.

The most prize-rich (and, to this writer, the most enjoyable) combat shotgun match is the annual Second Chance event. Write for information to Richard Davis, Second Chance, P.O. Box 578, Central Lake, MI

Competition's prime advantage is that it requires performance on demand under pressure. Several gunfight veterans have claimed that they felt more stress at a big match than they did in some of their violent encounters. The subconscious knowledge that "I performed before under tension with a gun in my hand" can be a life-saver. Competence and confidence are a best drawn as a circular pattern, feeding into and off of one another. Those who say competition is irrelevant to real-world performance tend never to have had the courage or confidence to try it.

Claybird shooting builds handling familiarity, but different shooting technique dynamics are needed for real-world training. Here 3-gun champ John Shaw dusts a clay bird with his Choate assault-stocked Remington 1100 12-gauge. Photo courtesy John Shaw, from his excellent shooting manual, "You Can't Miss."

A set of Remington 12-gauges with 26" barrels, Choate magazine extensions and assault stocks, and other match paraphernalia. Long barrels, unweildy for combat search, can have advantages in ensconced defender situations.

165

The legendary Jim Burnett strafes down a line of eight pins; notice that he's about to shoot the third while the first two are falling. Right-to-left swing worked for this rightie shooter; gun was Remington 1100 20 gauge, and Jim is able to stay upright without needing to lean forward against the mild recoil.

1991: Tom Mason presents Ayoob with Mossberg 500 Combo Kit as prize for winning 3-gun aggregate at Northeast Regional Pin Championship, Danbury, CT. Author holds the gun he used for shotgun stage, a borrowed, factory-stock Mossberg 500 pump. Photo courtsey TANSTAAFL Gun Club.

Shotguns are coveted prizes at combat shooting matches. John Bianchi presents author with deluxe Remington 870 12-gauge for his top-15 placement at 1979 Bianchi Cup Invitational.

Shotgun is key to many mixed-gun events. This prize-winning team in "Rolling Thunder" event at Second Chance circa 1979 was, L-R, Jim Baynes (Colt .45 Pistol), John Lazzaro (Remington 1100 12-gauge auto) Mas Ayoob (Commando carbine) and Jim Burnett (20-gauge Remington 100). Photo courtesy Second Chance.

By 1990, 4-man "Rolling Thunder" had evolved into 3-man team match at Second Chance: one shooter with pistol, one with pump shotgun, one with autoloading shotgun.

Chapter 22

Speedloading the Combat Shotgun

The author feels the most efficient way to deal with a shotgun that has run empty in combat is to follow the example of "Doc" Holliday in the OK Corral shootout: dump the empty gun and instantly draw your loaded handgun and continue firing.

This may not be possible if the shotgun is your only defensive weapon. It may not be necessary, if hostilities have been terminated and you merely need to "top off" your weapon to full load to cover the area, or to go forward with reinforcements to secure the scene.

It is also possible that you may have to rapidly load, as opposed to reload, a shotgun. This would be the case if you had to break out stored weapons to deal with a fast-breaking riot, in prison or on the street. It also relates to the armed citizen whose household rule is that no weapons will be kept loaded inside the home.

The oldest and most widely taught speedloading method for the shotgun is the one developed by the FBI. Its strength is that, in a pure timeclock sense, it is quick, and also that it allows you to cover the danger zone with at least one round loaded from very early in the procedure. However, it is quite fumble-prone and does not stand up well when the human factors of stress enter the picture.

Following along with the accompanying photos will show the strengths and weaknesses of what might be called the "Old Speed Reload." In OSR-1, the shotgun has run dry. My right hand is holding it

169

on target as the weak hand reaches for a shell. Note the unnatural angle of the wrist; even with the elbow tucked down and with this lightweight Remington 1100 LT-20, this is a difficult and awkward procedure.

OSR-2 shows that the shell is palmed in the left hand, its primer toward the shooter. It is now (OSR-3) slapped into the open shell port on the side of the weapon. Note that this will not work with the solid receiver of a bottom-ejecting shotgun such as the Ithaca model 37.

The bolt is now closed (OSR-4). This is done with the

thumb on the bolt release button on this Remington auto; with a pump shotgun, the forward hand would grasp the slide and drive it forward.

Still holding the gun on target with the dominant, rearward hand, the shooter now loads more shells in the magazine, weak-handed, by feel (OSR-5).

Problems are clearly evident. We are asking the weaker, less dextrous hand to work alone and "blind" in a time of great stress. The dominant hand's position holding the gun on target is unnatural and awkward, and may be impossible for those with limited arm strength.

It is for these reasons that LFI developed a more natural and positive technique for quickloading the shotgun. It might be called the "New Speed Reload" (NSR), and would go as follows.

As soon as the need to load/reload is perceived, the forward hand comes back to the receiver (to prevent hand being burned on hot barrel). Gun is now very solidly grasped and balanced (NSR-1) and the dextrous, dominant hand is free to manipulate the fresh shells. Note there is no pretense of covering a danger

zone with a raised but empty weapon.

The shell is dumped into the chamber (NSR-2) and the action instantly closed into a ready, firing battery (NSR-3). This will generally result in a gun loaded with at least one shell and ready to return fire sooner than will the old FBI technique, since the dominant

hand's strength and especially dexterity allow it to work more positively at greater speed.

The gun is now turned upside down, with muzzle slightly up (NSR-4). Looking past the shotgun, shooter has clear view of danger zone but can instantly glance down to rectify any problem that comes up as loading

continues. Note that use of strong hand allows shells to be loaded two at a time for much greater speed.

Throughout the procedure, we notice, the gun is held in an upside down version of "international skeet ready." If danger threatens, the gun can instantly be flipped into a

proper, effective two-hand firing position (NSR-5).

2-At-A-Time Shell Insertion

Utilization of the dominant, dextrous hand to manipulate the ammunition supply makes it possible to load two shells at a time into the magazine tube. This saves a great deal of wasted movement and, therefore, a lot of precious time.

In the past, many who tried to reload two shells at a time dropped so many rounds they gave up on the technique. This was because they were doing it incorrectly. Most of the time, they would place two shells in the hand, with the thumb holding them both against the fingers. However, the thumb must be used to force each shell into the tube securely past the shell stoppers. As soon as this was done with the first shell, the thumb was no longer securing the second against the fingers, and it would fall to the ground.

We discovered a more efficient technique for StressFire shooting. Hook the index finger and middle finger of the dominant hand into curved pincers (NSR-6). Two shells are now "stacked" there, held the way you would hold a cigar between those fingers (NSR-7).

Insert first one, then the other. As the thumb forces the first into place, the pincer-like fingers hold the second securely in place

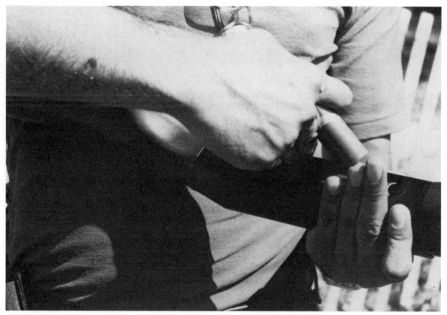

(NSR-8). The movement is the same for both shells.

The shell lifters of many shotguns function as "flippers" that require the shells to be forced past them. This is particularly true of the unmodified Remington 1100/11-87 series, in which a locking button must be depressed before the "flipper" can be bypassed. The technique shown is amply powerful enough to do this with the shell itself instead of a separate finger movement. The technique is also strong enough that it can be accomplished on the run, as seen in NSR-9, where the author is using a LaRocca Custom 1100 12-gauge Magnum fitted with extra shell carriers by L.L. Baston.

It should be noted that all depictions are for illustration of the technique. All tactical loading should be done behind cover. If he was caught in the open with an empty shotgun in real life, author would have drawn his loaded pistol and moved toward cover.

Chapter 23
Pistol Grip Only Shotguns

Strong arguments can be made between pistol grip assault stock, left, and conventional stock, both shown on Benelli Super 90.

Pistol grip only design reduces overall length, as does shortened barrel in this case, but also greatly reduces ability to deliver effective fire under stress. Ithaca 12-ga. m/37s are shown.

When compactness for storage is an issue, author strongly recommends folding stock rather than pistol grip only. Folding and fixed Remington 870s are shown for comparison.

Depending on individual, hip-level body position index can be achieved with bent forward arm, demonstrated by Paul Dewey with Ithaca Stakeout . . .

. . . or locked forward arm, demonstrated by author with Mossberg 500.

Raising firing hand to pectoral level and locking inside of wrist in hard is strong technique, will often (but not always) bring gun muzzle up into cone of tunnel vision.

Canadian constable learns the inefficiency of the pistol-grip-only 870 he was issued. He lines up for the first shot . . .

. . . and only after hitting low is able to adjust muzzle level for next shot. In real life, would he have had time for the second?

After pistol grip only shotguns were forced on his men, trainer Terry Campbell made the best of a bad lot. Here he shows techniques for such weapons at American Society of Law Enforcement Trainers seminar, Kansas City, MO 1989.

Pistol grip only 12-ga. can be fired one handed, but it's something of a stunt and wrist injury is possible.

When barrel is shortened toward pump handle, care must be taken to prevent forward hand from slipping in front of muzzle after recharge stroke. This was approach taken by Secret Service armorer Ray Steele on Secret Service Remington 870s with folding stocks.

NYPD Stakeout Squad developed hand sling on pump of Ithaca 37 to prevent dangerous forward hand overtravel with 14" barrel shotguns. Squad never used pistol grip only shotguns, but slide handle hand sling feature is seen on Ithaca's Stakeout models in both 12 and 20 gauge.

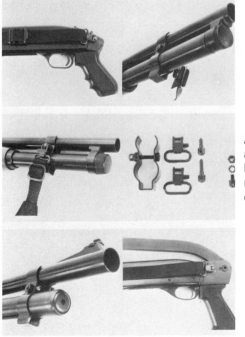

All the design modifying accessories shown here can be helpful in certain situations, author maintains, except for "pistol grip only."

181

Chapter 24

Tactics and Training

The purpose of this text is to learn *techniques* of controlling the combat shotgun. *Tactics* are a separate discipline entirely, and are not treated directly in this text. Certainly, the two concepts overreach one another's borders. For example, use of cover is a *tactic*, but successfully carrying out that tactic requires proper *technique,* as shown in this book's chapters on how to fire the shotgun from cover with maximum downrange effect and minimum exposure.

There are several schools that the author can recommend that teach good tactics in addition to his own Lethal Force Institute. They include Ray Chapman's Chapman Academy in Columbia, MO; John Farnam's Defense Training, Inc.; Louis Auwerbuck's Yavapai Firearms Academy; and many more. Pick up a current copy of COMBAT HANDGUNS magazine. This publication carries ads for most schools, with current phone numbers to call for details and this year's schedules. Many of these schools will have off-campus programs convenient to your region.

The following material illustrates some of the tactical aspects of defensive combat shotgunning that can be picked up at a good seminar or even a competitive tournament.

Shorter barrel shotguns are easier to deploy from inside vehicle. This is 14" barrel Ithaca.

Jim Gregg developed these steel silhouettes for combat training. A roller quickly spreads grease over the target to cover hits for next trainee.

Ray Chapman demonstrates running with shotgun, in this case a combat-modified 12-ga. 1100. It is critical to keep finger clear of trigger guard. Chapman Academy photo.

Bowling pins are good training for shotguns, but care must be taken to use heavy pellets and prevent angled fire, say Second Chance range officials.

Student learns "shooting on the move" with Bushmaster .223 "assault pistol." With shotgun, at least at slow speeds, a "step and drag" pace might be superior.

. . . and instantly mounts the gun and shoots the "identified threat" target. Absent cover or concealment, great speed is necessary.

Four different approaches to "entry problems." Ray Chapman slaps open door during simulated room search, his Benelli 121 in High Ready . . .

Same problem, different angle and tactic. With Benelli already mounted, Ayoob has rammed open door with gun muzzle and instantly shoots "identified threat." However, forward momentum has still carried him away from cover and concealment. Chapman Academy photos.

If door can be flung open, officer may be able to retain at least partial cover from doorway, and shoot like this student who is practicing standing barricade at falling plates, one shot per call. Against true multiple opponents, he would shoot right to left from right barricade position to reduce body exposure. Note puff of lead dust from 8" plate, center.

NYPD Emergency Services Unit officers practice door entry. Lead officers will fling battering ram forward and dive prone, drawing their sidearms, as the two officers behind them employ their shotguns from standing or standing barricade positions.

Deploying dash-mounted shotgun to react fo frontal threat. John Farnam comes to a stop . . .

Chambers a round and swings shotgun to left barricade position . . .

. . . and can fire instantly from where he is . . .

. . . or drop to a maximum low cover position and issue a challenge. Shotgun is Ithaca SKB 12-ga. autoloader.

2-hand nature of shotgun limits ability to use pocket mirror search around corners, a technique author demonstrates during Officer Survival lecture. For lone officer, handgun would give greater versatility in moving or searching mode.

Ordinary walking movements allow one to be constantly ready to fire with a light-kicking gun like the .223 Ruger Mini-14 author demonstrates to students here. However, he'd be off balance for the powerful recoil of a 12-gauge, and step and drag technique would better serve with the more powerful shotgun.

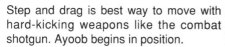

Step and drag is best way to move with hard-kicking weapons like the combat shotgun. Ayoob begins in position.

Forward leg steps deep, carrying body in forward direction.

Rear leg is "dragged" in same direction to complete the step, which can be repeated as needed. Body has throughout been in strong position to control a hard-kicking weapon in extreme rapid fire.

Gun is in low ready position throughout.

Felon's eye view of "pie-slicing." Good guy is minimum two steps back from corner, and with gun mounted on side that will first be exposed, edges out carefully bit by bit to check what's on the other side. Note minimal body exposure: loose vest is visible, but torso is behind cover.

Weare (NH) police officer Rick Devoid shows how StressFire Star technique, originally developed for handgun, can adapt to combat shotgun. A southpaw, he begins in conventional kneeling, facing 12 o'clock.

By simply pivoting to his weak side, Devoid can easily engage to 2 or 3 o'clock.

193

Continuing same movement (clockwise for left, counter-clockwise for right hander) and raising hips for better body rotation, Devoid can pivot in kneeling and shoot to 6 o'clock.

To cover the other sphere of the threat, that is going toward strong side, Devoid simply brings up knee down and down knee up. This allows a full sweep of strong side and combines with previous movements to give full 360° circle of fire from kneeling position. Note that with knee opposite gun shoulder down, shoulder must be aggressively forward into the weapon to maintain balance against rapid 12-ga. recoil.

Some schools suggest using bottom edge of butt as only contact point of stock to shoulder. Author does not care for this technique.

Seen from both sides, Front Snap technique as demonstrated by Officer Rick Devoid is extremely quick for emergency first shot, though pumping for subsequent shots may be slowed down. Strong tension in arm muscles is required to maintain control and prevent injury to shooter; crush grip is likewise necessary.

Roll-out from close cover position is demonstrated. Gun is mounted in shoulder pocket and brought up to line of anticipated target from kneeling position.

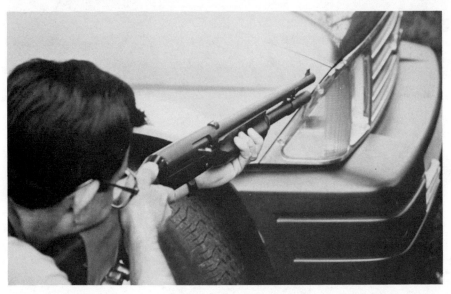

Body then rocks out from behind cover, firing as soon as clear sight picture is on opponent. Note that muzzle is barely clear of front of van in this photo. In this position, gun will tend to slip down toward brachial juncture between shoulder and bicep if shooter does not concientiously train to prevent it.

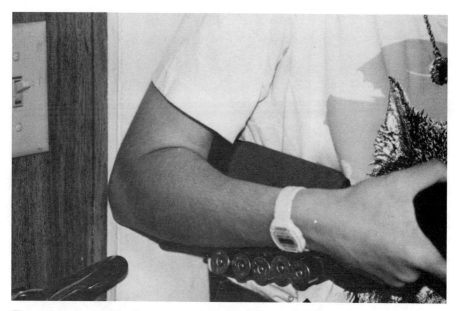

The pain-free Charlie Reese technique, already "street proven," is at its best in home defense scenario. Defender in dry-fire determines where to place butt against *solid* (not sheetrock) wall to have it in line with any window or doorway through which felon may enter. Butt is pressed firmly against support.

Tiny (100-lb) Rhonda Wilcox can now fire 8 12-gauge Magnums from author's Benelli with no pain, having wrapped herself around the stock in a high tuck position. BUTT IS AGAINST WALL, NOT SHOULDER. Bracing *shoulder* in this fashion could injure it; indeed, 12-ga. recoil is so powerful author has seen both stocks and wooden barricades broken just from live-fire training in this emergency position. Technique is extremely useful for the recoil-sensitive.